MW01483943

OUR FUTURE

ANGELENO
GROUP

with gratitude

Planeta

IVÁN **DUQUE**

OUR **FUTURE**

A green manifesto
for Latin America and the Caribbean

 Planeta

Work edited in collaboration with Editorial Planeta – Colombia

Title: *Our Future*

© Iván Duque Márquez, 2024

Translation: Azzam Alkadhi
Cover photo: © Alamy stock images
Photo of the author: © Nicolás Galeano
Cover design: Planeta Arte & Diseño
Graphs Design: Carlos Mendoza

© 2024, Editorial Planeta Colombiana S. A. – Bogotá, Colombia

Derechos reservados

© 2024, Editorial Planeta Mexicana, S.A. de C.V.
Bajo el sello editorial PLANETA M.R.
Avenida Presidente Masarik núm. 111,
Piso 2, Polanco V Sección, Miguel Hidalgo
C.P. 11560, Ciudad de México
https://www.planetadelibros.us

First edition printed: April 2024
ISBN: 978-607-39-1574-8

Printed in Quitresa Impresores, S.A. de C.V.
Goma No. 167, Granjas México, C.P. 08400,
Iztacalco, Ciudad de México.
Impreso en México −*Printed in Mexico*

To Juliana Márquez Tono, my mother,
to whom I owe my love for the environment.
To María Juliana, Luciana, Matías and Eloísa,
with whom I enjoy every passing moment in nature.

The increase in CO_2 will cause global warming.
EUNICE NEWTON FOOTE (1856)

Climate change is caused by human activity.
SVANTE ARRHENIUS (1896)

An immediate reduction in greenhouse gas emissions is necessary if we are to stabilize the climate.
HOESUNG LEE, CHAIR OF THE INTERGOVERNMENTAL PANEL ON CLIMATE CHANGE (IPCC) (2020)

CONTENTS

FOREWORD 13
Andrew Steer, PhD

INTRODUCTION
Moving towards a green manifesto 17

1. How we got here 27
2. Climate crisis and the role of Latin America 65
3. Climate action laws and cabinets 81
4. Green taxonomy 89
5. 30 × 30 Designation of protected areas 101
6. Ocean and reef protection 113
7. Green economies 121
8. Debt-for-climate swaps and voluntary carbon
   markets 145
9. Energy transition and the green hydrogen path 153
10. Green transportation 163
11. Low carbon agriculture and sustainable livestock
    management 171

12. Family solutions, households making a difference, the circular economy 183

13. Biodivercities 191

14. Green entrepreneurship........................... 199

15. Legal frameworks and security to protect the environment.................................... 205

16. The participation of indigenous communities in environmental protection........................ 211

17. Biodivercitizens: a movement with new ethics 221

EPILOGUE
Our individual manifesto............................... 225

ACKNOWLEDGMENTS 229

BIBLIOGRAPHY 233

FOREWORD

Solving the twin crises on climate change and the loss of nature requires us to embrace two seemingly inconsistent truths. First, we must be honest about just how bad the current situation is. We face an existential moment in human history. We are losing the battle. Second, we need to be inspired by the new ideas, inventions, and behaviors that offer the chance to drive exponential positive change, delivering a future much better than today's. We *can* solve the problem.

This wonderful book captures both of these truths in compelling narrative, with the positive tipping point story building throughout the chapters so that by the time the reader arrives at the Epilogue: *Our individual manifesto,* she or he is ready to get out there and fight for the change we need!

Latin America has many lessons for a world needing new ideas. It was Latin America which summoned the world together in 1992 to the Rio Earth Summit. I remember feeling a sense of hope and commitment as I watched Heads of State from around the world signing the Biodiversity Convention, the Framework Convention on Climate Change, and their commitments to prepare national Sustainable Development Plans. Sadly, we didn't deliver well on those promises, but in the years since we've seen remarkable innovation, often with Latin America in the lead.

Ideas such as eco-tourism, debt-for-nature swaps, payments for ecosystem services and Bus Rapid Transit were all incubated and ground-tested first in Latin America. So too, the region has been a leader in carbon markets for nature, green taxation, and restoring pasture lands.

As President of Colombia, Iván Duque demonstrated that actions to address climate and protect nature don't need to involve a trade-off with economic momentum. He embraced the new economics of the 21st Century, which shows that smart action on climate and nature opens up new economic opportunities, spurs new technology, reduces risks and improves economic efficiency – which can lead to more and better jobs, healthier air and water, more livable cities, less congestion, and a brighter future.

In illustration of this vision, President Duque has been a powerful leader in the 30x30 movement – a vision to conserve 30 percent of land and sea by 2030. Together with a small number of other world leaders, he deserves great credit for the the historic decision of 197 countries to support the 30x30 pledge at the COP15 meeting of the Convention on Biological Diversity, in December 2022.

But more important than pledges, his Administration put in place the largest expansion of protected areas perhaps in any country anywhere, so that the 30 percent target will be reached many years early. Colombian citizens will be better off as a result.

Few, if any, presidents write influential books on climate change while in office, but Duque's *The Road to Zero* did exactly that, arguing for a rethink of the way we understand the economy. This new book paints on a broader canvass, describing the remarkable innovations in the LAC Region and proposing an inspiring path into *The Future.*

If the ideas proposed in the pages that follow were to be implemented, our children and grandchildren will be safer, healthier, and happier.

It's not too late!

Andrew Steer, PhD

President & CEO,
Bezos Earth Fund

Moving towards a green manifesto

We live in a time of unprecedented change, but also of great risk. Artificial intelligence (AI) has been increasing its ability to process levels of data and information in record times and volumes. It is even capable of programmatically attaining human-like analytical skills, thereby revolutionizing science and all forms of knowledge. Yet, alongside these transformations, which are indicative of the ingenuity of humans in transforming their environment, it seems that indifference, apathy, and even deliberate refusal to address unavoidable issues are leading us on a frightening and irreversible path towards climate catastrophe, owing to a lack of effective and coordinated action.

While new and more sophisticated forms of AI-based services are released every week, we are also getting shocking news about the climate crisis. We have lost over 70% of our wildlife in the last five decades; if the deforestation rate in the Amazon remains unchanged, the region will become a net emitter of greenhouse gases in less than a decade; the increase in sea levels threatens entire cities; the constant occurrence of natural disasters, a byproduct of extreme climate events, annihilates lives indiscriminately; the millions of migrants who try to escape from these hazards each year show us that the time for giving speeches and making promises is over. We have to make changes, and fast. Actions must be articulated, immediate, blunt, ethical, coherent, congruent, and unbiased.

It is also true that nowadays, there is more environmental awareness than ever before and that many countries, through their leaders, have taken on important pledges. It would also be accurate to say that society, businesses, media and academia are all tirelessly working on mechanisms that would lead us to carbon-neutrality by 2050. Despite these optimistic signs – unless something unexpected and perhaps miraculous happens – the goal of climate stabilization of 1.5 °C may not be reached. We have recently witnessed some of the hottest months since the existence of precise weather measurements.

The climate change debate is focused on political recrimination. Those countries that benefitted from greater economic development as a result of greenhouse gas emissions are being questioned due to the absence of decisive results in climate action, while developing

Book - Democracy in America

countries claim that bearing the costs of demanding climate action will make it more difficult for them to work on their poverty reduction efforts and attempting to keep high standards of economic growth. Those debates – perhaps Byzantine, given the global reality – must be overcome. The implication is that richer countries will have to support the Global South for their actions to be synchronized, as a mismatch between developed countries moving forward, and developing countries lagging behind will lead us nowhere (see figures 1 and 2).

Latin America is a region that has contributed very little to the climate crisis, and nonetheless is vulnerable and exposed to the devastating effects of extreme climate events. Latin America cannot afford to take its time to respond or be indifferent to the current scenario, all the more so if we consider the fact that our Latin American and Caribbean regions hold the largest concentration of biodiversity in the world. Likewise, we possess some of the main sources of freshwater – more than 70% of the world's *paramos* or high-altitude wetlands, the Amazon biome, a natural machine capable of capturing CO_2, and an unquantifiable wealth of coral reefs. We cannot ignore our abundant fertile soil which holds the potential for providing food security, as long as environmentally responsible agriculture can be achieved. In short: without Latin America and the Caribbean, it would be impossible to solve the climate crisis that is affecting the planet today.

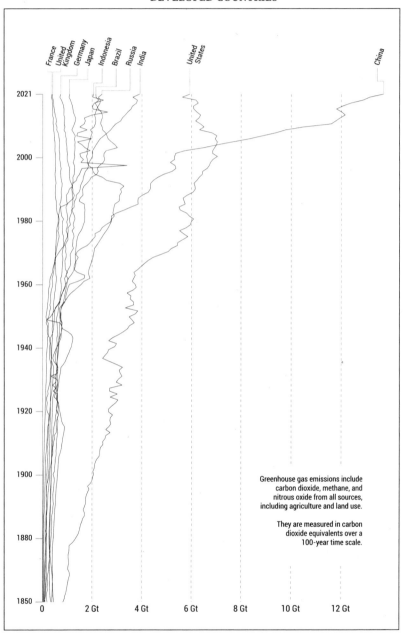

Greenhouse gas emissions include carbon dioxide, methane, and nitrous oxide from all sources, including agriculture and land use.

They are measured in carbon dioxide equivalents over a 100-year time scale.

SOURCE: GREENHOUSE GAS EMISSIONS - CALCULATED BY OUR WORLD IN DATA USING EMISSION DATA FROM JONES ET AL. (2023).

FIGURE 2 / CONTRIBUTION OF WORLD POWERS TO CLIMATE CHANGE

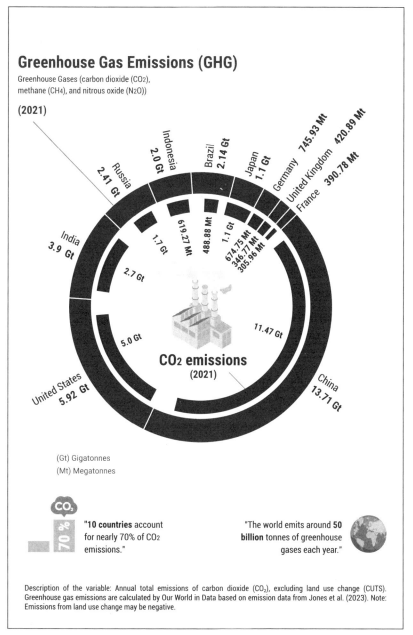

Greenhouse Gas Emissions (GHG)

Greenhouse Gases (carbon dioxide (CO2),
methane (CH4), and nitrous oxide (N2O))

(2021)

Russia 2.41 Gt
Indonesia 2.0 Gt
Brazil 2.14 Gt
Japan 1.1 Gt
Germany 745.93 Mt
United Kingdom 420.89 Mt
France 390.78 Mt

619.27 Mt
488.88 Mt
1.7 Gt
1.1 Gt
674.75 Mt
346.77 Mt
305.96 Mt

India 3.9 Gt
2.7 Gt
5.0 Gt
11.47 Gt

CO2 emissions
(2021)

United States 5.92 Gt
China 13.71 Gt

(Gt) Gigatonnes
(Mt) Megatonnes

"10 countries account
for nearly 70% of CO_2
emissions."

"The world emits around **50
billion** tonnes of greenhouse
gases each year."

Description of the variable: Annual total emissions of carbon dioxide (CO_2), excluding land use change (CUTS).
Greenhouse gas emissions are calculated by Our World in Data based on emission data from Jones et al. (2023). Note:
Emissions from land use change may be negative.

SOURCE: GREENHOUSE GAS EMISSIONS / CO2 AND GREENHOUSE GAS EMISSIONS • OURWORLDINDATA (2020).

Yet, given the role that our region has to play, there are a number of worrying asymmetries that can be seen. Our countries have taken on important climate pledges and have seen notable progress, but the high levels of debt, limited fiscal spaces, and the lack of significant private capital directed toward climate projects threaten the successful fulfillment of the objectives set for 2030 and 2050. Our countries must employ realistic, easy-to-finance, replicable, scalable and sustainable strategies as state policies, in which alliances between the private sector, civil society, communities, and minorities remain firm throughout.

To be successful and achieve results over time, we must have a logical framework and a minimum combination of actions. We require, on the one hand, a sort of *general manifesto*, that can be applied by every national and local government, which allows for joint efforts with private businesses, citizens and the international community; likewise, an *individual manifesto* is vital, which should be an easily applicable guide for people to use in their daily lives to help take care of the environment and mitigate climate change.

Given this double necessity, in these pages I propose a *green manifesto for Latin America and the Caribbean.* On one hand, it aims to act as a roadmap of actions to reach the goals that the countries have set. It will also attempt to put an end to the absurd ideological debates, full of prejudice, that intend to capture the political environment, generating paralysis and stagnation. On the other hand, the manifesto is designed for citizens to use in their everyday lives, to get information and ideas to help, however they can, to preserve nature.

This is a proposal that covers government coordination, regulatory frameworks, green financing, energy transition, carbon markets, sustainable agriculture, protected areas, eradication of deforestation, empowerment of the indigenous communities, urban planning with biodiversity in mind and, of course, a new green, circular, and responsible economy. This is a declaration of principles and actions, a combination of practical lessons that lead to palpable results and a roadmap for the homogeneity of action frameworks to put Latin America and the Caribbean front and center in the battle to protect the planet.

Many of the actions contained in *Our Future* have been implemented in Colombia and other countries in the region. Others are part of my experience from my period as president, as well as my desire to replicate effective measures from other places. The truth is that this is an urgent proposition which requires practical measures that leave no room for speculation. I lay the manifesto out with the intention for its application to be constantly improved upon and dispersed throughout the territory.

The reflections contained in these pages came from life experience and some wonderful multidisciplinary interactions at the University of Oxford, sponsored by the Development Bank of Latin America and the Caribbean (CAF) and the dean of the Blavatnik School of Government, Ngaire Woods, along with Professor Karthik Ramana, during my time as a fellow of this very important learning laboratory. The many hours spent on this research, the conversations with dozens of experts, and the interactions with the students themselves who challenged me with their intellectual curiosity about the necessary policies to face climate crisis allowed me to build this proposal in the most concrete, succinct, and practical way possible. I do not intend to make *Our Future* an exclusive, dogmatic or limited vision, nor do I intend to put this proposal forth as a presentation that nobody has made before. This is both a proposal and an invitation for countries to foster it, given that its application, with the possibility of further enhancing it, guarantees a foundation and expected results for the next few decades.

Climate action is neither right nor left-wing, it does not belong to a political, ideological, or religious party. It cannot be part of an electoral calculation, a card played by politicians during election times. In the face of the hazards that afflict the planet, care for the environment and actions aimed to mitigate the effects of climate change are the moral and ethical responsibility of every person. For that reason, it demands a great openness to dialog and cooperation, it requires teamwork among citizens, and between them and their leaders; it demands alliances between the private and public sectors, as well as the bidding of all the parties involved to find and support solutions based on nature. Without these fundamental aspects, it will be difficult to aim true, given that neither the state nor the private sector alone can solve the climate crisis.

Our Future is not exclusive to Latin America. Its structure and proposals are also applicable to countries in Europe, Asia, Africa, Oceania, and North America, on the logical premise that even among the most developed countries, many of the articulated actions have not yet been applied.

We are in a time that requires creativity, innovation, political will, social justice, entrepreneurship, and a collective awareness to save the planet from "global boiling", as recently coined by the current UN Secretary-General, António Guterres. *Our Future* is a bid for actions and results. If the proposals presented in this book are applied across all the countries of Latin America and the Caribbean, we will get to take one realistic step towards a green growth that is consistent with the objectives of sustainable development with the urgency that the world requires from us today.

Iván Duque Márquez
Oxford University, October 2023

1

How we got here

"C limate change is already here. It is frightening, and it is only the beginning. The era of global warming is over; the era of global boiling has arrived," said the Secretary-General of the United Nations, António Guterres, on July 27, 2023 (as cited by Aguayo, 2023); in addition to these words, he remarked at the United Nations General Assembly in September that same year: "We opened the gates of hell" (DW, 2023). The language he used simply confirms the urgency and the tone of the global situation we are experiencing, which has become the greatest challenge facing humanity in the last hundred years – an extreme extreme situation in which the very survival of our species on planet Earth is at stake. This is not an exaggeration. Climate change, a byproduct of greenhouse gas (GHG) emissions, has reached a point that is causing a tremendous impact across different spheres of society, perhaps irreversibly so. It is a phenomenon that can no longer be ignored, put on the back burner or seen as the exclusive responsibility of the governments in power. Sustainable development and the fight against climate change ought to be a quest led by citizens. It is through the sum of all their small actions that we can alter the course that is currently taking us head on towards a collective tragedy. The path of hope and positive outcomes ultimately begins with our change of attitude towards the environment.

The climate and environmental crises are real; neither is a minor occurrence nor a matter of speculation. Ever more frequently, we are witness to the consequences of uncontrolled and inadequate management of natural resources at the global and local levels. According to the reports of the United Nations Intergovernmental Panel on Climate Change (IPCC):

> Human activities, primarily through Greenhouse Gas Emissions, have unequivocally caused global warming, causing the temperature of the global surface to increase by 1.1 °C from 2011 to 2020, which was above the temperature recorded between 1850 and 1900. Global greenhouse gas emissions have continued to increase, with historically uneven contributions from the use of unsustainable energy, and the change in land use, lifestyles, and the patterns of consumption and production across regions, and among countries and individuals. (Inter-governmental Panel on Climate Change [IPCC], 2023).

In summary, the Earth's temperature today is 1.1°C higher than it was last century; it is the hottest temperature on record and the trend is that it will continue to rise. Every day, we wake up to the news that we are experiencing the most intense summers in several latitudes of the globe, causing deaths, droughts, forest fires and, paradoxically, more energy consumption to keep air conditioners and cooling systems running to cool the atmosphere inside the homes and offices in cities hit by heat waves. These unprecedented long and intense summers are accompanied by unseasonable downpours, floods and windstorms. This increase in temperature is scientifically proven; the damage it causes is becoming less and less imperceptible and is affecting, in one way or another, the lives and daily behaviors of *all* human beings.

In the same way, in countries where there are seasons, there have been extreme winters with record temperatures that have led to a growing demand for electric or gas heating systems. Climate change is not something sporadic or seasonal, nor is it something affecting certain places or populations. Every city, municipality or town is facing risks derived from global warming, which has prompted their respective authorities to create mitigation and response plans.

Global warming, that global boiling, is not only an increase in temperature; it also has implications that lead to harsh winters, with low temperatures and phenomena of previously unseen intensities. We have all experienced extreme weather conditions, environmental alterations of which there were no previous records, such as the melting of the Arctic ice, the rise in sea levels, coastal erosion, desertification, and natural disasters of enormous magnitude such as forest fires, droughts, tropical cyclones, floods, unprecedented hailstorms, cold fronts and prolonged winters, all caused by the increase in the temperature of our planet (see figure 3). As troubling as this situation is, it has shown us how weak and exposed the human species is to climatic alterations. We are vulnerable to diseases, some new and others old, but more acutely, to hunger and mass exoduses of people who can no longer live in certain rural areas due to food shortages, environments that are increasingly harsh, the lack of essential resources such as access to water, or work and dignified livelihood opportunities. Thousands of people are migrating to new urban centers that are beginning to form at the outskirts of large cities and are growing denser and damaging the environment in the process. However, these new urban centers have the potential to be better planned and thus have less impact on the environment, to become true *biodivercities* and perhaps the seed for a second chance on Earth for our species.

All of the above has brought economic, social and political consequences that can be perceived in people's daily lives. These are not matters reserved only for governments, politicians, businessmen or certain social classes: for the first time in history, each citizen can

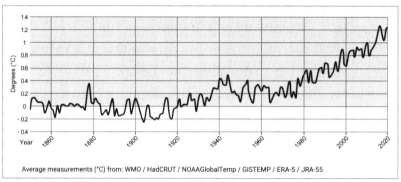

Average measurements (°C) from: WMO / HadCRUT / NOAAGlobalTemp / GISTEMP / ERA-5 / JRA-55

SOURCE: STATE OF THE CLIMATE IN LATIN AMERICA AND THE CARIBBEAN (2021)

contribute to the management and overcoming of a global crisis with small actions in our daily lives. No effort, no matter how small it may seem, will be superfluous for this purpose. It will take every one of us to ask ourselves if the actions we are taking will contribute to minimizing climate change or if, on the contrary, they will worsen the issue; it is imperative to create awareness of the fact that, by action and by omission, we are all partly responsible for this reality. There is time for adults to change their behavior, and we are also on time to encourage the very youngest children to protect the environment, from their first years of education at home with their families, so that these lessons can be reinforced at all levels of education. Fortunately, we already have a generation that makes its own consumption decisions and is not indifferent to this harsh environmental reality:

31

Concerned about the environment, the new generations have mobilized and generated an environmental revolution that we must all join. Young people understand that the real change is in our hands, and that it is up to us, human beings, to transform the climate reality we live in today. That is why they are so insistent that citizen culture must continue to evolve, giving greater priority to recycling practices, to being more conscious when buying -for example, clothes- and cultivating habits such as turning off lights that are not being used, to harness environmental resources in a responsible manner. (Duque Márquez, 2021, p. 34).

Environmentalist Paul Hawken, editor of the book *Drawdown: The Most Comprehensive Plan Ever Proposed to Reverse Global Warming* (2017), points out how the discussion on environmental protection must undoubtedly include regular citizens, without putting the entire burden of responsibility on them, and also how only together as a movement will we succeed in counteracting the enormous environmental impact.

To over-emphasize the individual can make people feel so personally responsible that they become overwhelmed by the enormity of the task at hand. Norwegian psychologist and economist Per Espen Stoknes has described how individuals respond to being besieged by science that describes climate change in a language of threat and doom. Fear arises and becomes intertwined with guilt, resulting in remaining passive, apathetic and in denial. To be effective, we require and deserve a conversation that includes possibilities and opportunities, not a repetitive emphasis on our ruin.

That conversation must extend beyond the individual, because any idea of us existing as isolated beings is a myth. Individuals cannot stop corrupt palm oil corporations from burning down Indonesia's rainforests, nor stop the bleaching and extinction of Australia's Great Barrier Reef corals. Individuals cannot prevent the acidification of the world's oceans or thwart the avalanche of advertisements dedicated to promoting desire and materialism. Individuals cannot stop the lucrative subsidies given to fossil fuel companies. Individuals cannot prevent this deliberate suppression and the intentional demonization of science and climate scientists by anonymous donors and the wealthy. What individuals can do is to become a movement. (Hawken, 2017, p. 206)

The only way to halt these dangerous and deadly effects is to rise up alongside this movement to bring greenhouse gas emissions to zero from a personal, family, neighborhood, and city-wide perspective, until a global movement is achieved. It is essential to create ways for all human activities to become carbon neutral and to be able to implement those that already exist and have demonstrated benefits in this direction. It is necessary to have a clear purpose and to:

> [...] recognize that as human beings, all our actions and ways of working and living together are emitting GHG. Therefore, the path is not to reach zero emissions, but to be able to neutralize them with our behavior and our creative capacity as soon as possible. In the same way that we aim to neutralize emissions, it is necessary to always have a path for the conservation and protection of nature in what we can call *carbon-neutral-nature-positive* actions. (Duque Márquez, 2021, p. 22)

Neither the most bitter global wars, nor the most prolonged economic crises have threatened the survival of humankind as much as the climate crisis has. This is a situation that is advancing so rapidly that we see the end of days for our human species as feasible and highly probable in the short term. We could even say that reality has begun to exceed fiction and that the movies that portrayed some possible version of the end of the world or of some parts of it due to a natural phenomenon are beginning to fall short compared to the destructive power of nature that we are seeing on a global scale. Simply put, nature is trying to find its own equilibrium in the midst of a great alteration caused for centuries by the hands of men. That is why halting climate change is an existential challenge that cannot be postponed and is not just a technical or scientific challenge. It is not something that will happen in the future; it is a present reality.

Currently we have access to more and better information about weather and natural phenomena. Climate studies have undergone meaningful transformation, from employing rudimentary methods to understand weather phenomena, all the way to applying sophisticated science to decipher our planet's complex patterns. In old times, climate studies were based on observations and anecdotal evidence of meteorological phenomena; civilizations such as ancient Greece and Rome had a rudimentary understanding of seasons and climate patterns. Over time, more precise measurement tools, such as barometers and thermometers, allowed for a better understanding of climate variables.

During the 19th century, the basis of modern meteorology was established and gave way to theories of atmospheric circulation and to the identification of global climate systems. In the mid-20th century, advanced technology such as satellites, radars, and meteorological stations paved the way for a more precise monitoring of climate events and meteorological forecasting. Throughout the 20th century, natural fluctuations in the weather were observed, including episodes of global warming and cooling. However, towards the end of the century, it became evident that human activities such as burning fossil fuels and deforestation were significantly contributing to global warming.

In the 21st century, climatology went even deeper into the study of climate change, caused mainly by human activity, and its impact. Extensive research has recorded continuous growth in global temperatures, the rise of sea levels, more frequent extreme climate events and changes in precipitation patterns. Nowadays, climate research is based on advanced computational models that simulate the behavior of the atmosphere and the ocean. Climate scientists study a variety of aspects such as the melting of glaciers, changes in sea levels, precipitation patterns, alteration of land and water ecosystems, and extreme climate events (hurricanes, storms, heatwaves, floods, among others). Also, international cooperation in data collection and the assessment of climate risks has made it possible to gain a global collective focus against climate change; collaborative scientific research has proven key.

Throughout the 21st century, technological advances related to climate analysis have revolutionized our capacity to understand and approach climate challenges. The integration of terrestrial observation satellites, remote monitoring systems with the use of radar and climate modelling technologies, have allowed scientists to obtain more accurate, real-time data about crucial climate variables, such as land surface temperature, sea level and wind patterns. In addition, high-performance computation has facilitated the compilation and analysis of *big data* such as large-scale climate models, which are ultimately helping us to forecast extreme climate events more precisely as well as to anticipate the effects of climate change. Likewise, this has fostered better emergency response by the emergency medical services as well as its growing professionalization.

Furthermore, Artificial Intelligencc (AI) has been key in the development of advances such as: climate predictions based on complex models and patterns; energy optimization to improve the generation and transmission of electricity; monitoring and conservation with the help of drones, surveillance cameras and real-time monitoring systems to prevent deforestation and poaching; optimization in the use of water, pest control and agricultural efficiency; solid waste management in landfills for its proper disposal and recycling; material design and eco-friendly processes; traffic management in cities; and planning to reduce GHG emissions. Additionally, clean transportation has been promoted along with the monitoring of the behavior of the ocean (temperature, water level, etc.) and its biosphere. Currently, the environmental impact of infrastructure projects and human activity are being assessed.

These technological advancements not only push scientific research forward, but they also provide support for decision-making processes regarding climate change adaptation and mitigation policies in all implicated aspects. As we will see and as has been demonstrated, there is no aspect in the life of any human being that is not connected to climate change.

Latin America, just like the rest of the world, experienced tremendous changes with Covid-19, including seeing how its productive activities came to a halt. We faced a kind of uncertainty that most generations – young, middle-aged, and even elderly people – had never been through. We had knowledge of localized plagues and epidemics. Maybe we thought those were distant and would never reach us, but we could have never imagined such a scale, as if we were part of a blockbuster film with special effects. Despite the fact that scientists and public health experts had been warning the population for decades about the possibility of pandemics caused by new pathogens, such as highly contagious viruses, the arrival of Covid-19 could not have been foreseen. Even though the world responded to the crisis and impressively managed to stop it and mobilize globally to vaccinate and protect the world in record time, the loss of life was inevitable, whether from the virus itself or the aftereffects in the human body.

In addition to the crisis caused by climate change, we also had to worry about the pandemic. Hundreds of thousands of people died, and this emotional impact made us reflect on the urgency of reconsidering the path that our societies were taking in environmental terms. We had to rethink the way we faced health emergencies and how governments could respond to protect their citizens (see figure 4).

FIGURE 4 / COMPARISON OF PEOPLE AFFECTED BY CLIMATE
CHANGE, INFECTED WITH COVID-19, AND DECEASED DUE TO
BOTH CAUSES

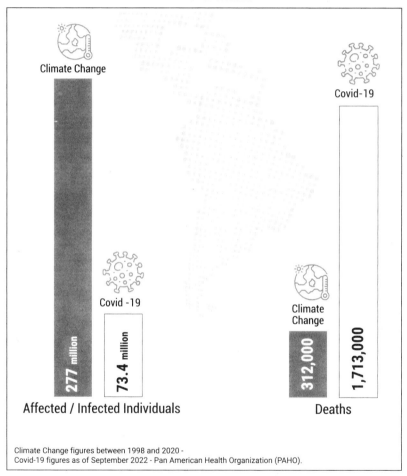

Climate Change figures between 1998 and 2020 -
Covid-19 figures as of September 2022 - Pan American Health Organization (PAHO).

SOURCE: REUTERS COVID-19 TRACKER - UNITED NATIONS.

Covid-19 made it even more imperative to change our economies, change many regular consumption habits, focus on conservation without leaving productivity aside and vice versa. Even if global warming itself did not directly cause the pandemic, there is evidence that climate change can influence the speed at which infectious diseases are spread. The rise in temperatures and the alteration in climate patterns can affect the geographic distribution of vectors, just like disease-carrying mosquitoes, which eventually leads to the spreading of vector-borne diseases, such as dengue or malaria.

Additionally, climate change can alter ecosystems, thus affecting the interaction between animals and humans; this could entail a faster spread of zoonotic diseases, like Covid-19. According to the research paper *Climate Change and the Covid-19 Pandemic* (Lacy-Niebla, 2021):

> Everything we consume impacts nature. Deforestation, agricultural development, and climate change are causing an increase in vector-transmitted diseases. The Covid-19 pandemic is the result of the disturbance caused by human activity in nature. In a large number of infectious diseases, the pathogen has lived inside another species before affecting humans. Such species have been key in their ecosystems for hundreds of years, but human intervention stops its transformation; by destroying certain components, an important imbalance is generated.

During the first days of the lockdown, we witnessed the rejuvenation of our surroundings, a substantial improvement in air quality, noise reduction, and the return of certain species to their natural habitats which had been previously usurped by human activity. We also noticed how weak our health system was, but in contrast, we realized that as a society we were strong and willing to help others; in fact, the real heroes of this period were doctors all around the world. Likewise, we witnessed how fragile our food supply chain was, with the scarcity of agricultural inputs and raw materials; the world economy slammed on the brakes, and we can still feel the aftermath today. The Covid-19 pandemic added one more element to the great environmental crisis, and it was clear how both phenomena were not isolated, as it changed the way we saw life, the way we saw the world, or at least we hope it did. As Bill Gates states in his book *How to Avoid a Climate Disaster* (2021):

> If you want to understand the kind of damage that climate change will inflict, look at COVID-19 and then imagine spreading the pain out over a much longer period of time. The loss of life and economic misery caused by this pandemic are on par with what will happen regularly if we do not eliminate the world's carbon emissions. (p. 49)

The argument and conclusion are terrifying: *the Covid-19 pandemic is but a sample of what is to come regularly if nothing is done to stop climate change.* However, despite how negative and disastrous the pandemic was, the silver lining is that we were able to seriously question our use and dependence on fossil fuels. We also saw alternative ways of performing regular, everyday activities like studying, working or doing research. As a species, we learned to socialize in other ways, to connect with each other in different ways. Unfortunately, it seems as though only catastrophic events, such as the pandemic and its effects on everyday life, can make us see how imminent the risks are. Nobody expected a pandemic to spontaneously develop, just as nobody expected to experience the effects of global warming so closely. Some were able to envision the crisis, but only the real visionaries could see the opportunities that it brings.

Can we face the climate crisis? Yes. Can we do it with solutions based on technology, innovation, and creativity? Solutions based on nature and respect for the environment? That is another yes. With the same zeal with which many human developments ended up affecting the environment, we can, all of us as a species, move towards resolution. Human beings have been able to create the worst weapons of mass destruction; we need to trust that the same inventiveness will now be focused on our salvation. We cannot face it individually; we need to stay united around the higher purpose of stopping what seems inevitable, above ideological, religious, social, philosophical, economic, or political differences. Climate change affects us all and we can start to mitigate its impact with the will to act as one – moving in the same direction. More than ever, individual and collective leadership will be essential for the sake of the greater good.

There are human actions that are turning into the largest source of greenhouse gas emissions in developing countries. Today, deforestation and the negative use of the land are generating around 20% of the GHG emissions on the planet. If those were a territory, it would be the second largest air-polluting country. To put it in perspective, that is the largest cause of emissions we have in Latin America and the Caribbean (see figure 5).

A question arises then: given its comparatively low emissions, what is the role of Latin America in this global emergency? In fact, there are some Latin American countries whose emissions as a percentage of their GNP are among the lowest compared to countries forming part of the Organization for Economic Co-operation and Development (OECD) (see figure 6).

So, if Latin America's contribution to GHG emissions is low compared to other regions, why should fighting climate change and global warming be a priority in our continent and specifically in the South American sub-region? Should it not be the most powerful and richest nations, which are also the ones who pollute the most and have contaminated the planet, who ought to come up with greater solutions and commit to making immediate change?

Figure 5 / Deforestation in Latin America

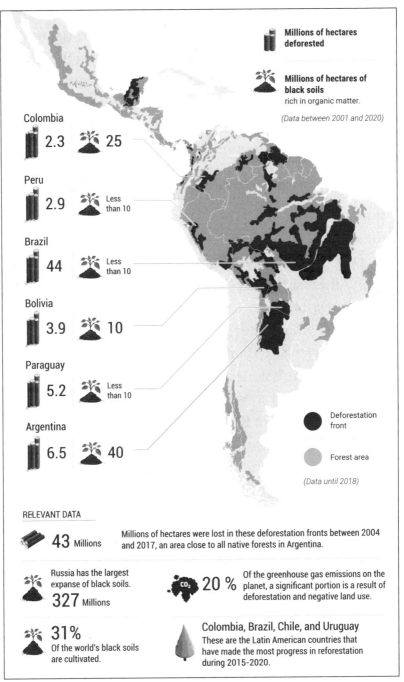

Millions of hectares deforested

Millions of hectares of black soils rich in organic matter.

(Data between 2001 and 2020)

Colombia
2.3 25

Peru
2.9 Less than 10

Brazil
44 Less than 10

Bolivia
3.9 10

Paraguay
5.2 Less than 10

Argentina
6.5 40

Deforestation front

Forest area

(Data until 2018)

RELEVANT DATA

43 Millions — Millions of hectares were lost in these deforestation fronts between 2004 and 2017, an area close to all native forests in Argentina.

Russia has the largest expanse of black soils.
327 Millions

20 % Of the greenhouse gas emissions on the planet, a significant portion is a result of deforestation and negative land use.

31% Of the world's black soils are cultivated.

Colombia, Brazil, Chile, and Uruguay These are the Latin American countries that have made the most progress in reforestation during 2015-2020.

SOURCE: DEFORESTATION IN THE AMAZONIA BY 2025 / RAISG / (2022).

Figure 6 / Greenhouse Gas Emissions in Latin American and Caribbean countries compared to OECD countries

Latin America and the Caribbean		/ OECD Countries	
Brazil	1469.64	5289.13	United States
Mexico	609.07	1062.78	Japan
Argentina	394.76	731.54	Canada
Colombia	270.31	681.18	Germany
Venezuela	237.63	613.54	South Korea
Peru	179.78	609.07	Mexico
Bolivia	131.43	585.42	Australia
Paraguay	97.29	476.34	Turkey
Ecuador	94.19	411.12	United Kingdom
Chile	49.69	339.21	Italy
Nicaragua	38.15	320.92	Poland
Guatemala	36.78	314.57	France
Cuba	35.62	256.41	Spain
Dominican Republic	35.50	162.55	Netherlands
Uruguay	34.28	102.64	Czech Republic
Honduras	27.67	100.27	Belgium
Trinidad and Tobago	26.61	83.75	Israel
Panama	21.46	70.86	New Zealand
Guyana	18.17	70.56	Greece
Suriname	13.54	66.46	Ireland
El Salvador	12.15	64.09	Austria
Haiti	10.9	61.7	Finland
Jamaica	7.58	61.39	Hungary
Costa Rica	7.08	56.01	Portugal
Belize	6.96	49.69	Chile
Barbados	3.65	43.19	Denmark
Bahamas	2.83	42.25	Switzerland
Grenada	2.40	34.95	Slovakia
Antigua and Barbuda	1.20	34.14	Sweden
Saint Lucia	0.70	31.33	Norway
Saint Kitts and Nevis	0.33	15.65	Slovenia
Saint Vincent	0.30	14.83	Estonia
Dominica	0.22	11.53	Latvia
		8.54	Luxembourg
		3.27	Iceland

Units in megatonnes of carbon dioxide equivalent
All GHGs including LULUCF = Land Use, Land-Use Change, and Forestry.

Source: Greenhouse Gas Emissions - Calculated by Our World in Data using emission data from Jones et al. (2023).

The answer is clear: Latin America has the leading role at this moment in history. We can be the continent that ignites hope amid global uncertainty; we can make the shift towards more sustainable societies before we reach the extremes of damage already experienced by other countries due to GHG emissions. A World Bank report (2022, Nov. 3) concluded that "low- and middle-income countries can make the transition to resilient, low-carbon growth models if certain key conditions are met with international support." From the Rio Bravo to Patagonia, we must build a path to zero emissions through a strategy that guides all Latin American citizens without exception in the pursuit of the achievements and goals that guarantee carbon neutrality. We can and must distinguish ourselves from the rest of the world through the quality of our policies towards nature; that is precisely the purpose of this manifesto: to set out specific actions towards carbon neutrality, positive conservation, and sustainability in our continent.

We need to develop what I have called *Sustechnability*, a creative blend of technology and innovation focused on achieving sustainable development in Latin America. We must move towards renewable energies with clean means of transportation. We need to stop deforestation and change consumption habits and production models, as well as building a new generation of green businesses based on the circular economy, payment for environmental services and nature-based solutions.

Innovation is not just about inventing new machines or processes, but also about devising new approaches to business models, supply chains, markets and policies all of which help inventions come to life and diffuse globally. Innovation is as much about new gadgets as it is about new ways of doing things. It is about developing new ways of approaching business models, supply chains, markets and policies that help inventions come to life and spread on a global scale. (Gates, 2021, p. 252).

Some will raise concerns as to why Latin America should make efforts in this direction if it contributes so little in terms of emissions; or why make such efforts when the budgets of our countries do not have the same kind of leeway as those of more developed countries who can invest in research and development into innovations in the environmental field. According to a recent report, *The Roadmap for Climate Action in Latin America and the Caribbean 2021-25*:

The region is responsible for 8% of global greenhouse gas emissions. The agricultural sector, along with changes in land use and deforestation, accounts for 47% of emissions in Latin America and the Caribbean, well above the global average of 19%. Energy, electricity consumption and transport account for another 43% of emissions (World Bank, 2022, Sep. 14) (see figures 7 and 8).

Figure 7 / Global Greenhouse Gas Emissions by Sector

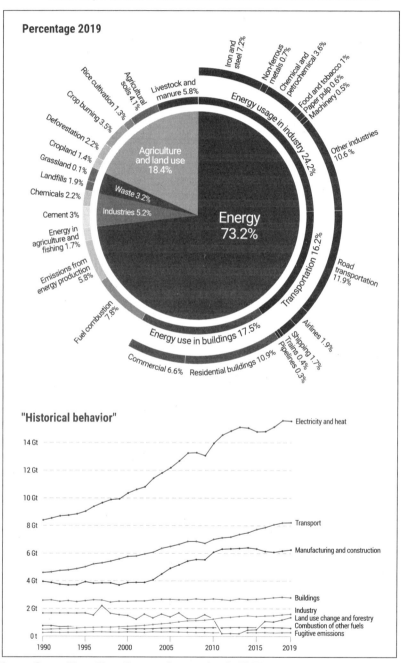

Percentage 2019

Iron and steel 7.2%
Non-ferrous metals 0.7%
Chemical and petrochemical 3.6%
Food and tobacco 1%
Paper pulp 0.6%
Machinery 0.5%
Energy usage in industry 24.2%
Other industries 10.6%
Rice cultivation 1.3%
Agricultural soils 4.1%
Livestock and manure 5.8%
Crop burning 3.5%
Deforestation 2.2%
Cropland 1.4%
Grassland 0.1%
Landfills 1.9%
Chemicals 2.2%
Cement 3%
Energy in agriculture and fishing 1.7%
Emissions from energy production 5.8%
Fuel combustion 7.8%

Agriculture and land use 18.4%
Waste 3.2%
Industries 5.2%

Energy 73.2%

Transportation 16.2%
Road transportation 11.9%
Airlines 1.9%
Shipping 1.7%
Trains 0.4%
Pipelines 0.3%
Energy use in buildings 17.5%
Commercial 6.6%
Residential buildings 10.9%

"Historical behavior"

14 Gt
12 Gt
10 Gt
8 Gt
6 Gt
4 Gt
2 Gt
0 t

1990   1995   2000   2005   2010   2015   2019

Electricity and heat
Transport
Manufacturing and construction
Buildings
Industry
Land use change and forestry
Combustion of other fuels
Fugitive emissions

FIGURE 8 / GREENHOUSE GAS EMISSIONS BY SECTOR IN LATIN AMERICA AND THE CARIBBEAN (2022)

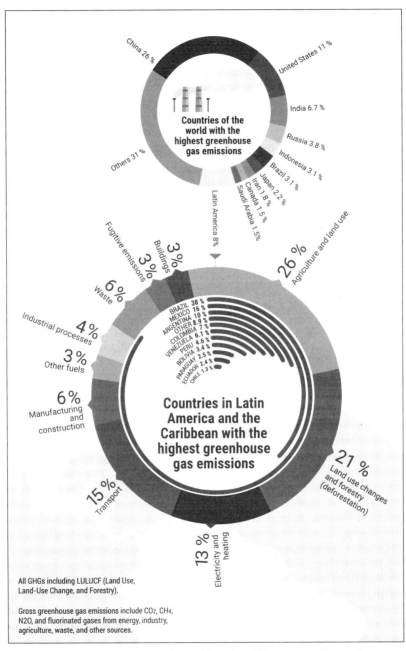

SOURCE: HISTORICAL GHG EMISSIONS FROM CLIMATE WATCH. (2022). WASHINGTON, DC: WORLD RESOURCES INSTITUTE.

This is reiterated in the third chapter of the *Regional Economic Outlook for Latin America and the Caribbean: A Long and Winding Road to Recovery* entitled "Climate Change in Latin America and the Caribbean: Challenges and Opportunities", by several researchers when they state that:

> LAC [Latin America and the Caribbean] is one of the most diverse regions in terms of climate risks. Neither Brazil nor Mexico stand out in terms of net GHG emissions per capita, but both countries, along with Argentina, contributed more than one percent to total net GHG or non-CO_2 net emissions globally in 2018, just because of their sheer size. LAC is also home to countries that are particularly vulnerable to the impact of climate change (especially in the Caribbean and Central America), and countries that do not contribute substantially to global GHG emissions but are sensitive to transition risks (i.e., exporters of fossil fuels and agricultural products). Climate change is of critical importance to the region from a macroeconomic point of view and both climate mitigation and adaptation are relevant (International Monetary Fund, 2021) [see figure 9].

Along the same lines, another report called *State of the Climate in Latin America and the Caribbean 2021* points out:

FIGURE 9 / AMOUNT OF GHG AND CO2 EMITTED PER PERSON IN LATIN AMERICA AND THE CARIBBEAN (2022)

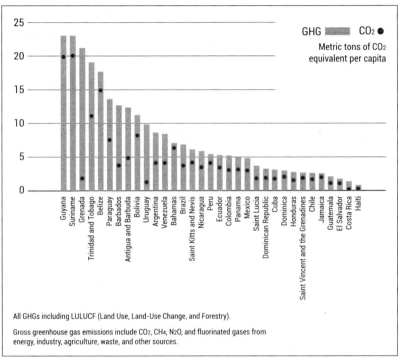

All GHGs including LULUCF (Land Use, Land-Use Change, and Forestry).

Gross greenhouse gas emissions include CO2, CH4, N2O, and fluorinated gases from energy, industry, agriculture, waste, and other sources.

Source: Historical GHG emissions from Climate Watch, World Resources Institute (2022).

Latin America and the Caribbean is one of world´s regions most affected by climate change and external weather phenomena that are causing serious damage to health, life, food, water, energy, and socioeconomic development in the region. The report notes that climate-related events and their impact have claimed over 312,000 lives in Latin America and the Caribbean and affected more than 277 million people between 1998 and 2020. (IMF cited by Mora, 2021)

It is true that our continent faces some of the greatest inequalities in the world and that there are priorities to be addressed in our populations such as access to health, education and even food security, which must be solved first. However, if we change the way we look at these issues, we will realize that they are also intimately related to climate change mitigation. There is no social problem today that does not fall under the umbrella of the climate crisis. The same report states that:

Latin America is projected to be one of the regions of the world where the effects and impacts of climate change, such as heat waves, reduced crop yields, forest fires, depletion of coral reefs and extreme sea level events will be most intense. The report is forceful in assuring that limiting global warming to below 2.0 degrees Celsius, as dictated in the Paris Agreement, is vital to reducing risks in a region that already faces economic and social asymmetries for its sustainable development. (Mora, 2021) [See figure 10]

In this regard, I believe that this vision compels us to give priority to addressing the climate crisis and seeing it as the backbone that will help to solve other problems afflicting our societies, and to achieve at least a 45% reduction in GHG emissions by 2030 and carbon neutrality across most Latin American countries by 2050. In summary, all national or local government programs in Latin America that aim at solving the critical and immediate problems of our societies, such as health, education, access to food, and national security, must take into account a broader vision which incorporates the environment at its core, leading to other actions in each specific area. In other words, there can be no state policy that ignores an environmental component, not as a formal requirement, but as its very source of inspiration. Every public policy must consider how it will help mitigate climate change both in application and execution because there are no areas that are exempt from the emergency that we are experiencing as a species.

This takes on a special meaning in Latin America because we have the greatest biodiversity in the world. In this continent, we have the Amazon biome, which is as large as the United States and represents the greatest biodiversity per land unit in the world (see figure 11).

FIGURE 10 / IMPACT OF CLIMATE CHANGE ON THE SPREAD OF DISEASE IN LATIN AMERICA

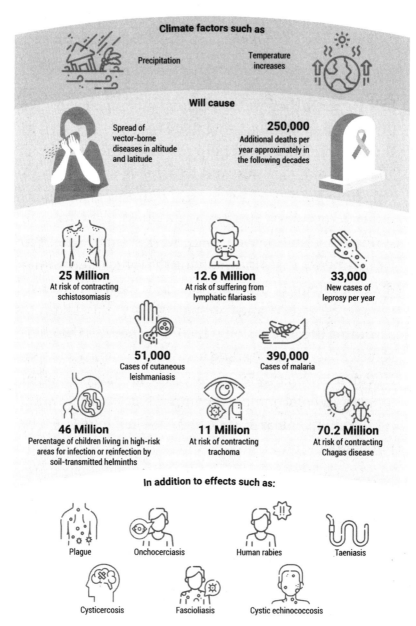

SOURCE: WORLD HEALTH ORGANIZATION - UNPRECEDENTED PROGRESS IN THE FIGHT AGAINST NEGLECTED TROPICAL DISEASES REPORT (2017).

FIGURE 11 / THE AMAZON IN NUMBERS

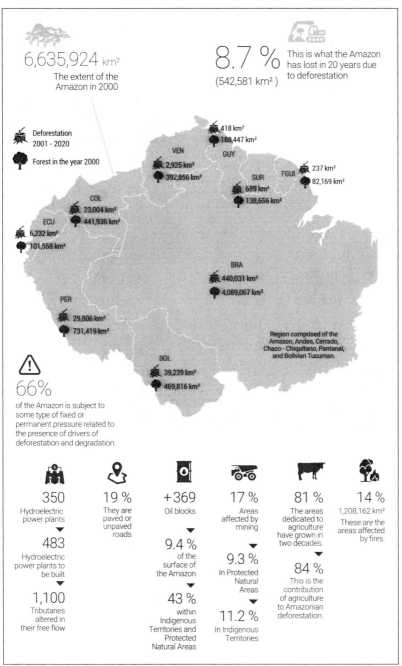

6,635,924 km²
The extent of the
Amazon in 2000

8.7 %
(542,581 km²)
This is what the Amazon
has lost in 20 years due
to deforestation

Deforestation
2001 - 2020

Forest in the year 2000

418 km²
188,447 km²

VEN
2,925 km²
392,856 km²

GUY

SUR
689 km²
138,656 km²

FGUI
237 km²
82,169 km²

COL
23,004 km²
441,936 km²

ECU
6,232 km²
101,558 km²

BRA
440,031 km²
4,089,067 km²

PER
29,806 km²
731,419 km²

Region comprised of the
Amazon, Andes, Cerrado,
Chaco - Chiquitano, Pantanal,
and Bolivian Tucuman.

BOL
39,239 km²
469,816 km²

66%
of the Amazon is subject to
some type of fixed or
permanent pressure related to
the presence of drivers of
deforestation and degradation.

350
Hydroelectric
power plants
▼
483
Hydroelectric
power plants to
be built
▼
1,100
Tributaries
altered in
their free flow

19 %
They are
paved or
unpaved
roads

+369
Oil blocks
▼
9.4 %
of the
surface of
the Amazon
43 %
within
Indigenous
Territories and
Protected
Natural Areas

17 %
Areas
affected by
mining
▼
9.3 %
In Protected
Natural
Areas
▼
11.2 %
In Indigenous
Territories

81 %
The areas
dedicated to
agriculture
have grown in
two decades.
▼
84 %
This is the
contribution
of agriculture
to Amazonian
deforestation.

14 %
1,208,162 km²
These are the
areas affected
by fires.

SOURCE: DEFORESTATION REPORT IN THE AMAZONIA BY 2025 - AMAZONIAN NETWORK OF GEO-REFERENCED SOCIO-ENVIRONMENTAL INFORMATION.

Latin America is at the crossroads of climate change, facing longer droughts, more intense hurricanes and storms, landslides and floods. Phenomena such as El Niño and La Niña occur periodically, but with increasing strength and intensity; these are affecting more people as a consequence of global warming. According to the World Bank, nations should "invest an average of 1.4 % of gross domestic product (GDP) per year [to] reduce emissions in developing countries by 70 % by 2050 and increase resilience" (2023, Nov. 3).

If we understand *resilience* as "the three conditions that enable a social or ecological system to absorb change and, fundamentally, not collapse: the ability to self-organize, the ability to mitigate disturbances and the capacity to learn and adapt" (Glemarec, 2011, p.10), it will be a key word in this whole effort, always linked to another: *restoration.* In fact, it is the planet itself, its rivers and ecosystems, that show us their enormous capacity for self-recovery and resilience, but their self-regenerative quality is not infinite and has been abused.

To mention just one of the aspects which we should be most proud of: Latin America contains approximately 23% of the world's forests (Economic Commission for Latin America and the Caribbean [ECLAC], 2021), 57% of which are primary forests that can capture an estimated 104 gigatons of carbon from the atmosphere, and are home to between 40 and 50% of the world's biodiversity and a third of all the planet's plant species. Yet the

Amazon River basin, which stretches across nine South American countries and captures 10% of all the world's carbon, has been exposed to fierce deforestation over the last four years due to forest fires and clearing of the forest to adapt the land for livestock farming (World Meteorological Organization (2021).

Between 1990 and 2020, the share of regional forest cover decreased steadily from 53% to 46% of the territory. While at the beginning of the 1990s, the region's forest area covered some 1.07 billion hectares, by 2010 it had shrunk to 960 million hectares, and by 2020 it had decreased to 932 million. Therefore, the total loss of area covered by forests in the region between 1990 and 2020 amounted to 138 million hectares, equivalent to a little more than the entire surface area of Peru or half the size of Argentina. (ECLAC, 2021).

Furthermore, Latin America is home to more than 70% of the high mountain ecosystems, known as *paramos*-moorland-style reservoirs of pure water; Latin America is home to the greatest wealth of coral reefs in the entire planet; and we have a variety of fauna and flora that makes us stand out on the world stage. We are – all of Latin America – a powerhouse of biodiversity and natural resources; it is our greatest asset. Therefore, not only would it make sense for every public policy to contain "the environmental issue" as its main goal, but that it should be our inspiration, our guiding principle; that the conservation, protection and preservation of natural resources should be, if not the main objective, then one of the fundamental purposes. We need to recover the vision and sensitivity of our indigenous ancestors, who had a close relationship with nature because it was part of their life. They did not conceive Earth as a source of resources to extract or trade. In their cosmogonies, any damage to the Earth was an attack against their mother; it meant harming themselves. The Western vision views the planet as a source of resources and a series of ecosystems to be dominated for our own benefit. Indigenous peoples, however, strive to maintain communion with the Earth; for this reason, they did not destroy it or take advantage of its enormous capacity for recovery. They took what was necessary, thus creating and preserving the natural cycles while enjoying the resources in a healthy and respectful manner.

All Latin American public policies ought to involve both institutional and civilian actions and focus on: environmental conservation; the protection of ecosystems, resources and species; the protection of the traditional knowledge of those who have been the guardians of nature since before the arrival of the Spanish to the Americas; and the promotion of innovation and research with a single purpose, the protection of life and species. Only through the sum of the contributions of each sector in each country will a significant reduction of emissions be achieved. Each citizen, young and old, regardless of their origin or social condition, will play an essential role in this process.

Latin America has the unique ability to unite two concepts: *carbon neutrality* and positive conservation. The union of these two is what we have called *The Road to Zero*, one that will lead us to fulfill the seventeen Sustainable Development Goals (SDGs) (figure 12).

The challenge is to reduce greenhouse gas emissions by at least 45% by 2030 and to achieve carbon neutrality in the vast majority of the region by 2050, in accordance with the SDGs. This requires reaching a consensus and a certain balance, because it is not through dogma or ideological impositions that we are going to solve these issues, but rather through documented, planned, inclusive and democratic actions.

Issues such as deforestation or contamination from mercury and other substances in the rivers that flow through the continent's terrain must be combated continuously. According to the document *The State of Biodiversity in Latin America and the Caribbean: An assessment of progress towards the Aichi Biodiversity Targets*:

> In many parts of Latin America and the Caribbean, mining activities cause the release of pollutants such as mercury from gold mining and "red sludge" from bauxite mining into the environment. It has been estimated that more than 13 million cubic meters of water with dissolved toxins are released into freshwater ecosystems each year from mining and metal-related operations. Similarly, oil and gas industries are also a major source of water

FIGURE 12 / MILLENNIUM DEVELOPMENT GOALS

1 ERADICATION OF POVERTY

End poverty in all its forms throughout the world.

2 FIGHT AGAINST HUNGER

End hunger, achieve food security and better nutrition, and promote sustainable agriculture.

3 GOOD HEALTH

Ensure healthy lives and promote well-being for all ages.

4 EDUCATION QUALITY

Guarantee inclusive, equitable and quality education, and promote lifelong learning opportunities.

5 GENDER EQUALITY

Achieve gender equality and empower all women and girls.

6 DRINKING WATER AND SANITATION

Ensure the availability and sustainable management of water and sanitation for all.

7 ENERGIES RENEWABLES

Guarantee access to affordable, safe, sustainable and modern energy for all.

8 DECENT EMPLOYMENT AND ECONOMIC GROWT

Promote sustained, inclusive and sustainable economic growth, full and productive employment, and decent work for all.

9 INNOVATION AND INFRAESTRUCTURAS

Build resilient infrastructure, promote inclusive and sustainable industrialization, and foster innovation.

10 REDUCTION OF INEQUALITY

Reduce inequality within and between countries.

11 CITIES AND COMMUNITIES SUSTAINABLE

Make cities and human settlements inclusive, safe, resilient and sustainable.

12 CONSUMPTION RESPONSIBLE

Guarantee sustainable consumption and production patterns.

13 FIGHT AGAINST HIM CLIMATE CHANGE

Take urgent measures to combat climate change and its effects.

14 FLORA AND FAUNA AQUATI

Conserve and sustainably use oceans, seas and marine resources for sustainable development.

15 FLORA AND FAUN TERRESTRIAL

Protect, restore and promote sustainable use of terrestrial ecosystems, sustainably manage forests, combat desertification, halt and reverse land degradation and halt biodiversity loss.

16 PEACE AND JUSTICE

Promote just, peaceful and inclusive societies.

17 ALLIANCES FOR THE ACHIEVEMENT OF OBJECTIVES

Strengthen the means of implementation and revitalize the global partnership for sustainable development.

SOURCE: UNITED NATIONS

contamination (United Nations Environment Programme [UNEP] & World Conservation Monito- ring Centre [WCMC], 2016, p. 63).

Similarly, it is important to understand that there is an urgent need to address aspects such as the energy transition, although many countries in the region still rely heavily on resources coming from hydrocarbons and the mining energy sector, which will be difficult to replace overnight, as is the case of Colombia. Bill Gates (2021) cautions as follows:

> Finally, in communities where coal or natural gas extraction is an important part of the economy, people will understandably be concerned that the transition will make it difficult for them to make ends meet. The fact that they express this concern does not make them climate change deniers. One does not have to be a political scientist to reason that national leaders who advocate the need to go to zero will gain greater support if they understand the concerns of families and communities whose livelihoods will be severely affected and take them seriously. (p. 240)

In such conditions, rigorous and careful change must be made without jeopardizing the economic balance and sustainability of our societies, especially that of the most vulnerable populations. The ability to change is within our reach, perhaps now more than ever before, but this cannot become a catch-all and empty phrase. Certainly, we must not delay in meeting the challenges posed by climate change, but it is not with lavish and messianic speeches that we are going to change the course of the world's climate change. It is through state policies that are exercised responsibly by elected leaders, and not as individual acts whose merit is attributed to the ruler of the day. Moreover, these policies ought to respect the constitution and the rule of law, protecting, above all, nature and the sustainability of society. We need change through action, not just words and not under a capricious political banner. Change is accomplished through coordinated effort, not by intentions alone, no matter how good these may be. Karen Armstrong says in her book, *Sacred Nature* (2022):

> The cause of this crisis lies in the characteristics of modern existence, which, despite its considerable achievements, suffers from fatal flaws. We are beginning to realize that the present habits in our way of life, even with their many benefits, are not only inhibiting the flourishing of the human race, but are threatening the very survival of our species. It is not enough to change our lifestyle; we must also change our entire belief system. If we have plundered nature, treating it as a mere resource, it is because over the

past 500 years we have cultivated a worldview very different from that of our ancestors (p. 15).

In Latin America, this is deeply relevant because our territory is home to centuries-old cultures whose philosophy of life has been the friendly and harmonious coexistence with the environment. We need to recover their legacy in order to continue along the path of carbon neutrality, in which steps have been taken, but they are incipient and there is still a long way to go; moreover, we must travel this path working together as much as possible. This global crisis is our opportunity to set an example, as a region, of how to confront this great existential challenge with what we have, both in terms of wealth and shortcomings. We must understand that we have challenges to overcome through specific actions in each country and must implement them to establish ourselves as a green power in the world. If we are successful, we may be able to showcase the power of carbon neutrality and positive conservation as a banner that is not flaunted by any particular leader or political current, but rather one that each Latin American citizen can fly as their own.

2

Climate crisis and the role of Latin America

Climate change has left a deep mark on Latin America. Its effects are greater here, due to the weakness of our social fabric, the limited resources for proper emergency response, fragile infrastructure, insufficient support networks as well as the challenging geography of our territories, mainly characterized by the Andes Mountain range, the savannas and grasslands, and the rainforests. Our idiosyncrasy as Latin Americans has also shaped the way in which the gravity of global warming has been understood and the way it has been handled, both by governments, and on a daily basis by citizens. However, before we go any deeper into the aforementioned aspects regarding climate change, let us get a glimpse of some of the consequences left by climate change in our region.

Rise in temperatures

Data from the CCCP – Pacific Oceanographic and Hydrographic Research Center (2022) – shows that the average temperature in Latin America has increased by around 0.8 °C between the start of the twentieth century and the 2010s. This increase has been especially accelerated in the last few decades, with an annual increase of approximately 0.2 °C in some countries (see figure 13).

Extreme climate events

According to *The Roadmap for Climate Action in Latin America and the Caribbean 2021-25*, "Latin America and the Caribbean are some of the regions that are most vulnerable to the destructive power of these types of phenomena. The interruptions to the energy and transportation infrastructure systems end up costing an equivalent of 1% of the region's GDP and up to 2% in some countries of Central America" (World Bank, 2022, Sep. 14).

FIGURE 13 / TEMPERATURE ANOMALIES IN LATIN AMERICA AND THE CARIBBEAN

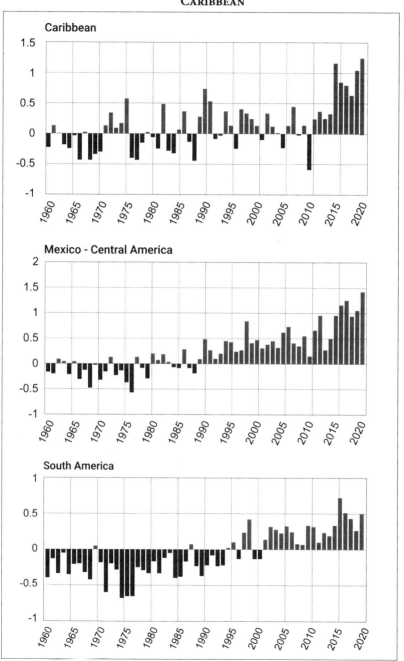

Source: World Meteorological Organization - Report on the State of the Climate in Latin America and the Caribbean (2021)

Declining biodiversity and water contamination

According to the *Biodiversity Status and Trends of Biodiversity in Latin America and the Caribbean* Report published by the United Nations Environment Program (UNEP), the region has lost close to 30% of its biodiversity since the beginning of the 20th century. In some countries like Brazil or Colombia, this number is even higher, at a 50% loss (UNEP & WCMC, 2016) (see figure 14). Water contamination has affected aquatic species, food production, and human health.

Rising sea levels and loss of coastal ecosystems

According to the World Meteorological Organization in its *State of the climate in Latin America and the Caribbean* report: "The sea level in the Latin America and Caribbean region has increased at a higher rate than the global mean especially along the South American Atlantic coast south of the equator (3.52 ± 0.0 mm per year, from 1993 to 2021) as well as the Subtropical North Atlantic and the Gulf of Mexico (3.48 ± 0.1 mm per year, from 1993 to 1991)" (ECLAC, 2022, Jul. 22). In the same way, the loss of vital ecosystems such as coral reefs and mangroves, due to global warming, has affected the natural balance.

FIGURE 14 / WATER POLLUTION IN LATIN AMERICA

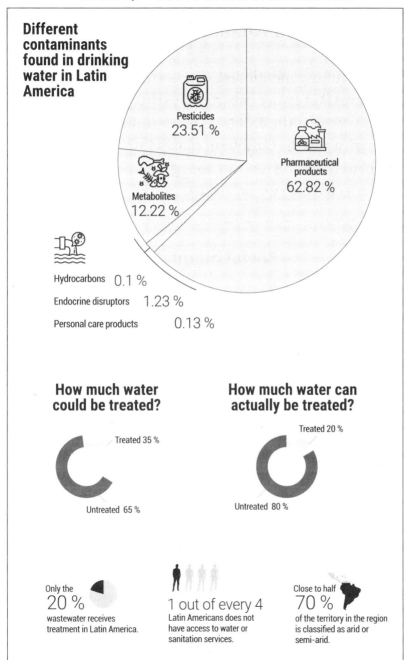

Different contaminants found in drinking water in Latin America

Pesticides
23.51 %

Pharmaceutical products
62.82 %

Metabolites
12.22 %

Hydrocarbons 0.1 %

Endocrine disruptors 1.23 %

Personal care products 0.13 %

How much water could be treated?

Treated 35 %

Untreated 65 %

How much water can actually be treated?

Treated 20 %

Untreated 80 %

Only the
20 %
wastewater receives treatment in Latin America.

1 out of every 4
Latin Americans does not have access to water or sanitation services.

Close to half
70 %
of the territory in the region is classified as arid or semi-arid.

SOURCE: SUSTAINABILITY, EFFICIENCY, AND EQUITY OF WATER CONSUMPTION AND POLLUTION IN LATIN AMERICA AND THE CARIBBEAN (2015).

Economic impact

As previously mentioned, most of the natural disasters that are taking place have stemmed from climate change. According to the ECLAC, "natural disasters in Latin America and the Caribbean cause close to 7 billion USD in material losses, and an average of 4.5 million people are affected every year" (CEPAL, 2009).

Social inequality

People with the lowest incomes are the most vulnerable to the consequences of climate change. This occurs in part due to the scarcity and price surges of food as well as potential issues related to access to water supplies. As a result, phenomena such as internal migration of communities in search of daily sustenance is not uncommon. One of the economic consequences of Covid-19 was the widening gap between the wealthy and the poor, exacerbating their already deteriorating life conditions as a result of the lack of access to resources (see figures 15 and 16).

FIGURE 15 / NEW DISPLACEMENTS IN LATIN AMERICA DUE TO NATURAL DISASTERS IN 2020

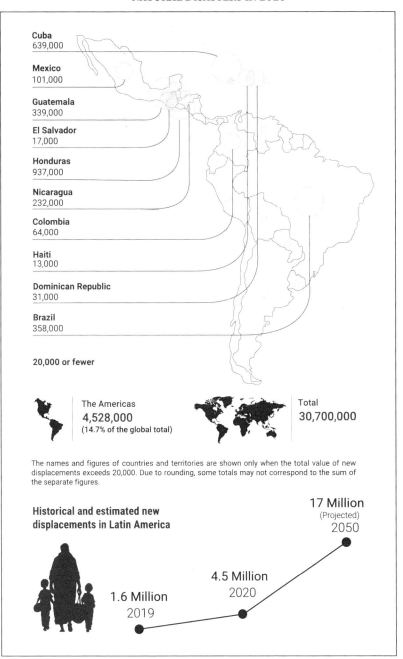

Cuba
639,000

Mexico
101,000

Guatemala
339,000

El Salvador
17,000

Honduras
937,000

Nicaragua
232,000

Colombia
64,000

Haiti
13,000

Dominican Republic
31,000

Brazil
358,000

20,000 or fewer

The Americas
4,528,000
(14.7% of the global total)

Total
30,700,000

The names and figures of countries and territories are shown only when the total value of new displacements exceeds 20,000. Due to rounding, some totals may not correspond to the sum of the separate figures.

Historical and estimated new displacements in Latin America

17 Million
(Projected)
2050

4.5 Million
2020

1.6 Million
2019

SOURCE: INTERNATIONAL ORGANIZATION FOR MIGRATION (IOM).

FIGURE 16 / NEW DISPLACEMENTS IN THE WORLD BY DISASTERS: BREAKDOWN BY THREATS (2008-2020)

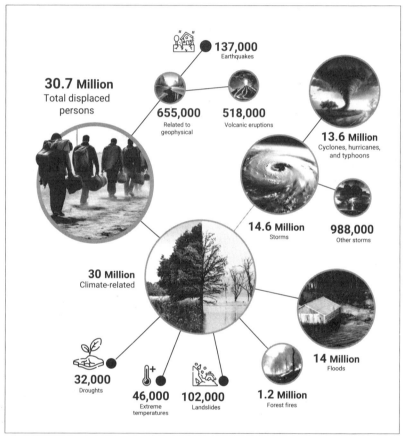

SOURCE: INTERNATIONAL ORGANIZATION FOR MIGRATION (IOM)

Agriculture at risk

Agricultural productivity in Latin America could decrease by up to 50% by the end of the 21st century, due to higher temperatures and unpredictable rainfall patterns. Agriculture is also one of the activities that, if left unchanged, will affect environmental conditions. According to The Nature Conservancy:

> So far, the contribution of almost a quarter of said emissions resulting from agricultural production and deforestation had been overlooked. Industrial agriculture uses a third of the unfrozen land surface and close to two-thirds of the global water resources. Above all, monocultures such as soy, used for both animal feed and energy generation, are laying waste to forests, which are natural carbon sinks. These and other agricultural practices are degrading the soil, which is being lost 10 to 100 times faster than it is being regenerated. Desertification and degradation of ecosystems caused by agricultural production amounts to a loss of a forest area the size of Sri Lanka every year (Studer, 2019).

Increase of vector-borne diseases

The Pan American Health Organization (PAHO) and the World Health Organization (WHO) have reported an increase in diseases such as dengue and zika in Latin America, caused by climate change, given that warm and humid conditions promote the proliferation of disease-transmitting mosquitoes. According to these international bodies, "climate change fuels some threats to health, and creates new public health challenges. Just by analyzing a few health indicators, 250,000 additional deaths will take place per year in the coming decades as a result of climate change (PAHO & WHO, s. f.)." According to a 2021 report by the International Monetary Fund (IMF):

Latin America and the Caribbean (LAC) is one of the most diverse regions with respect to climate-related risks. While Brazil and Mexico do not stand out in terms of per capita net greenhouse gas (GHG) emissions, each of these countries, together with Argentina, contributed more than one percent to total net GHG or net non-CO_2 emissions globally in 2018 simply due to their sheer size. LAC is also home to countries that are especially vulnerable to the impact of climate change (notably in the Caribbean and Central America), and to countries that do not contribute significantly to global GHG emissions but are sensitive to transition risks arising from global efforts to reduce GHG emissions (i.e., fossil-fuel and agricultural exporters). The region's net GHG emissions are in line with its economic size and population, so that per capita net GHG emissions of 6.4 metric tons CO_2 are close to the world average (FMI, 2021).

Latin America is a diverse and complex region that spans a large part of the American continent, from Mexico in North America all the way down to the Southern Cone at the south end of South America. With a population of around 659 million people, Latin America is home to a mix of cultures, languages, and ethnicities. Its population is characterized by its youth, with an average age of 29, lower than many other regions. This poses multiple challenges and opportunities in terms of education and labor (United Nations Population Fund, UNFPA). Latin America makes up approximately 8% of the global population, now over 7.8 billion people. This places it as the fourth most populous region in the world, just after Asia, Africa and Europe.

From an economic perspective, Latin America is home to some of the largest economies in the world, such as Brazil and Mexico. However, it also faces important economic challenges, including income inequality. Additionally, its dependence on raw material exports, such as oil, minerals and agricultural products, has led to a certain vulnerability to the fluctuations of global commodities prices.

Throughout its history, Latin America has experienced constant changes in terms of politics. During the 20th and 21st centuries, the region witnessed several political systems, from stable democracies to authoritarian dictatorships. The latter have been oppressing their people under the flag of a misunderstood type of socialism. We have seen democratically elected governments being targeted by attempted coup-d'etats or elected presidents trying to launch internal coups. We have seen the pendulum of ideologies move from extreme to extreme, polarizing societies and institutions, while critical issues such as climate change have been steadily escalating in the background.

In environmental terms, Latin America is known for its exceptional biodiversity, which includes vast tropical jungles, imposing mountains, and diverse coastlines. However, the region also faces environmental issues, such as deforestation, the loss of natural habitats and contamination. The conservation of these natural resources is essential, not only for global biodiversity, but also for the wellbeing of the local communities. *The Roadmap for Climate Action in Latin America and the Caribbean 2021-25*, by the World Bank Group (WBG), has identified three high-priority systems as well as two cross-cutting areas as a framework for action against climate change.

HIGH PRIORITY SYSTEMS

• *Landscapes, agriculture, and food systems:* Improving the management of our landscapes, agriculture, and food systems offers key opportunities to generate resilience in the face of climate change, and at the same time, reduces emissions with carbon sequestration. Climate-intelligent agriculture, sustainable use of the land and water resource management are essential, both to achieve net zero emissions, and to guarantee long-term productivity in groups of natural resources that satisfy the growing market demand for agricultural products which do not promote deforestation and generate low-carbon emissions instead.

• *Energy and transportation systems:* Focusing on achieving more resilient assets and networks in the face of climate change. Also, decarbonizing energy generation, transportation systems and manufacturing of goods. Avoiding dependency on infrastructures that make intensive use of carbon by incentivizing private sector investment for low carbon-emission solutions. This could drive growth and productivity, and, at the same time, help accomplish the GHG mitigation commitments.

• *Cities:* Up to 80% of total losses caused by natural disasters in Latin America and the Caribbean take place in urban areas, which also produce one third of the GHG emissions on a regional scale. Managing cities to attain greater resilience in the face of climate events and implementing decarbonization of urban systems is a priority for climate action. Achieving this can also help cities become more efficient, thus favoring their development and the wellbeing of their citizens.

CROSS-CUTTING AREAS

• *General economic actions:* determining the governmental, financial, and institutional conditions to respond to climate change from an economic standpoint. This can be achieved by reducing financial and economic risks, by promoting decarbonization and by approaching the challenges of the economic transition with low carbon emissions.

• *Supporting vulnerable populations:* Focusing on the protection of the people who are most vulnerable to climate events and addressing the risks of energy transition. It is essential to guarantee their participation in the decision-making process for climate action. (World Bank Group, 2022, p. 5)

There are multiple necessary and urgent efforts that need to be made. Time goes on and it is unrelenting; climate change and global warming are unyielding. Just as this crisis took place progressively, the way in which it can be managed and held at bay will be the sum of multiple actions aimed at slowing down the alarming numbers. If done properly, and in the long term, the current conditions may improve and go back to far less dire conditions. That is why in my upcoming lines, I will attempt to describe the actions that, from my perspective, are necessary to mitigate the crisis in Latin America. Some of these actions are related to institutional aspects and others to the daily lives and efforts of regular citizens.

Latin America is in an ideal position geographically, economically, and socially to lead the fight against climate change for multiple fundamental reasons. First, the region is rich in natural resources, and it possesses exceptional geographical and biological diversity. From the Amazon rainforest to the vast deserts, Latin America possesses a multitude of ecosystems that offer unmatched opportunities for the development of innovative systems of clean energy. The abundance of renewable energy sources, such as solar, wind, hydroelectric, and geothermal, places the region in a strategic position to achieve a transition to an economy with little to no dependence on carbon.

Furthermore, Latin America is home to a diverse and multicultural population, which includes indigenous and Afro-descendant communities with a deep and ancestral knowledge of the sustainable management of natural resources. These communities have historically demonstrated commitment to and respect for nature, ultimately playing an essential part in the protection of local ecosystems. Their active participation and sustainable practices can enrich and strengthen regional efforts to fight climate change.

Additionally, Latin America is experiencing sustained economic growth as well as investment in infrastructure leveraged on multilateral financial mechanisms, which can aid in the adoption of clean technology and sustainable environmental practices. The expansion of sectors such as renewable energy, sustainable transport, and waste management can not only reduce the emissions of greenhouse gases, but also create jobs and attract international investment.

To summarize, the region possesses a wealth of natural resources and cultural diversity, as well as the capacity to develop innovative clean energy systems, and use the wisdom of its indigenous and Afro-descendant communities to achieve sustainable management of resources. The sum of these elements can place the region as a potential leader in the fight against climate change and the task of promoting a more sustainable future for the globe; now, we just need to turn rhetoric into action.

3

Climate action laws and cabinets

A growing coalition of nations has reached consensus around reducing their greenhouse gas emissions by at least 50% on average by 2030. Commitment levels vary among countries with some pledging to higher percentages and earlier deadlines than others. Some less optimistic voices have already cast doubt on targets being met. Some countries have already postponed their deadlines to 2050. That said, in a world where differences, polarization and debates reign, having reached a consensus is an enormous step forward, and the fact that 70 countries have committed to this goal is also a hopeful prospect in an increasingly volatile, uncertain, complex and ambiguous world. *The Emissions Gap Report 2022* states:

> [...] the commitments made by governments to date have fallen short of what is needed. Current national climate plans for the 193 signing parties of the Paris Agreement

would lead to a significant increase of almost 11% in global greenhouse gas emissions by 2030, compared to 2010 levels. (United Nations Environment Programme [UNEP], 2022).

These transnational commitments require each state to act locally to determine and promote the necessary legal frameworks and allow the execution of actions that will endure over time, beyond national or local government administration periods. As stated before, confronting this climate crisis transcends any ideology or political party.

Committing to achieving specific environmental targets and indicators on the international stage requires the creation of laws that support climate action and its implementation in each country. More specifically, each of these laws must take into account the contribution of each productive sector in the reduction of emissions. Citizens, public and private entities, authorities, and local and national government agencies require a stable and reliable legal framework within which to operate, and which prioritizes environmental conservation above all else. Under this legal framework, every individual in our society will know that their actions, however small, should be aimed at conserving the environment or, at the very least, not negatively affecting it.

It is fundamental to coordinate public policy with the commitment of citizens to ensure that we are, above all, caring for the resources of a planet that is becoming extinct. This must be talked about over and over at home, in schools and universities, in private companies and, of course, within the public sector. In each of these spaces, there should be permanent training in environmental care and carbon footprint mitigation, defined as follows:

> [...] the total amount of greenhouse gases emitted as a direct or indirect effect of an individual, organization, event or product. While there are many ways to look at the measurement of Carbon Footprints as a tool to mitigate climate change, as well as to create guidelines and solutions. [...] it is the Carbon Footprint of products that has the greatest relevance and impact in the short term in Latin American countries since they are exporting primary agricultural and mining products, and some more elaborate ones. Thus, the analysis of different national strategies ought to be considered, including all dimensions of carbon footprint: territories, companies, sites, products and services. (United Nations Economic Commission for Latin America and the Caribbean - ECLAC, 2010).

All of us – individuals, groups, public and private companies, regardless of origin, class, race, religion or ideology, line of work or economic activity – are responsible for preserving our resources, but it will be difficult if there is no permanent flow of information or reminders of their importance. Caring for the environment is the conviction that should bring us together; the survival of our species is the highest purpose that should unite us.

Establishing the Nationally Determined Contributions (NDCs) was a major step in this direction, as they "embody each country's efforts to reduce national emissions and adapt to the effects of climate change" (UNEP, n.d.). These resulted from the signing of the Paris Agreement on December 12th, 2015, which came into effect on November 4th, 2016. This agreement got 194 parties (193 countries plus the European Union) to commit to "reducing their emissions and working together to adapt to the impacts of climate change" (United Nations [UN], n. d.). Also, it determined that every five years all nations of the world would take on increasingly ambitious targets and set the framework for developed nations to trade paths not only to mitigate their emissions, but to help underdeveloped nations reach their targets. "In their NDCs, countries communicate the actions they will take on to reduce their greenhouse gas emissions in order to achieve the goals of the Paris Agreement. Countries also communicate in these NDCs the measures they will take on to build the resilience needed to adapt to the impacts of rising temperatures" (UN, n. d.).

NDCs are voluntary commitments that countries make to address climate change and reduce greenhouse gas (GHG) emissions on a national level. They are a set of goals, targets and measurements that each country establishes in order to decide what actions it will take to reduce its emissions and adapt to the effects of global warming, taking into account its own national context, its capacities and economic development.

NDCs can include a variety of elements, such as GHG emission reduction targets, climate change adaptation measures, financial and technological commitments, and plans to strengthen national climate action capacity. It is important to note that NDCs are not necessarily linked to a specific time period, which means that some countries may set long-term targets, while others may opt for short-term commitments. Countries commit to review and improve their NDCs periodically, usually every five years, with the aim of bolstering their efforts to overcome climate change.

Countries also commit to providing clear and transparent information on their NDCs, as well as to regularly report their progress on implementation of proposed measures. This allows each country's efforts to be globally monitored and helps maintain accountability.

For many developing countries, effective implementation of their NDCs will require financial and technical support. The Paris Agreement recognizes the importance of providing such assistance to ensure that all countries, regardless of their economic capacity, can effectively address climate change. For each country to achieve its NDCs, internal coordination is required and therefore, it is essential to have "climate action cabinets" in each of the Latin American countries. These should promote GHG reduction standards in their sectors and monitor their compliance not as individual pieces of a puzzle, but as essential axes for the fulfillment of a purpose that, as we have said, not only belongs to each nation, but to the region and to humanity as a whole.

Climate action cabinets are the coordinating bodies that push for action, monitor goal fulfillment and aim towards specific results in each subsector in order to meet the larger objective. Public officials, regardless of their levels of responsibility, ought to set an example by keeping environmental care as a guiding principle in their daily public affairs. Following suit, an even higher standard of burden for setting an example in the way they pursue actions to mitigate the causes and effects of climate change ought to fall on heads of state. The responsibility of a head of state in this matter today is immense: it requires coherence and an enormous dose of realism to confront the climate crisis with facts and data instead of empty illusions, since what they have in their hands is not a game, but rather the very survival of the societies they govern.

It is natural that disputes arise in the creation of climate action cabinets, especially when resources are scarce, as they happen to be in most Latin American countries, due to the different allocation of budget to each sector. Therefore, the head of state should have the possibility of creating climate action cabinets led by the presidency, in which all ministries and officials involved in these goals can permanently track and follow up on the contribution of each specific sector. Despite disputes, collaborative and innovative solutions to the greater purpose of overcoming the climate crisis must emerge. Along with "resilience", "innovation" – in the broadest sense of the term – will be another actionable word to overcome this crisis.

This does not require creating more red tape, entities or ministries, as these types of solutions to climate change may result in a waste of money. It is a matter of political will and, above all, of coordinating actions, monitoring implementation, and measuring progress judiciously with existing institutions. It's a matter of helping them adapt to a reality that is unavoidable regardless of which sector they operate in. There is no other way to achieve these global goals of sustainability and to fight against climate change; governments must begin by reviewing their way of acting locally, and by setting an institutional example for all citizens.

4

Green taxonomy

G reen taxonomies are classification systems that assess the environmental sustainability of certain economic activities; they have emerged as an innovative and powerful response to the climate crisis. Established by the European Union to boost sustainable investment, these tools have been embraced across Latin America to help guide decision-making in key sectors.

The institutional effort to have climate action cabinets must rely on the vital input of green taxonomies by country. These are glossaries of the environmental policies that a government is advancing, the objectives it intends to achieve and the mechanisms to measure results sector by sector. Taxonomies are public documents that are useful for capital markets or investors when they are deciding whether to invest in a given country. Having access to these classification systems gives credibility and confidence to investors in environmental issues because they know the degree of a country's commitment to combatting climate change. By guiding sustainable investments, tracking the actions to reduce carbon emissions and those that are used to enhance the compliance of international agreements, these tools help to stay the course on a path to a cleaner future. Latin America has the opportunity to lead the fight against climate change through Green Taxonomy, building a legacy that transcends generations and borders. According to *The Roadmap for Climate Action in Latin America and the Caribbean 2021-25*:

> Although green financing in Latin America and the Caribbean has grown significantly in recent years and has exceeded USD 1 billion in Brazil, Chile and Mexico in the last five years, it is not enough to meet climate and environment goals. Achieving the full potential of climate action across Latin America and the Caribbean can be accelerated through the development of green finance solutions, such as the adoption of sustainability standards, green taxonomies, system of monitoring, reporting and verification aligned with accepted sustainability standards, and the disclosure of the risks and achievements related to the climate by financial intermediaries and the business sector in general. (World Bank, 2022, p. 19)

However, the implementation of green taxonomies has its challenges, such as the need for more accurate data and collaboration among various government actors; overcoming these obstacles is crucial to maximizing the impact in Latin America and creating a legacy of climate resilience. I will now outline the most significant advantages of green taxonomy.

Flow of sustainable investments

Green taxonomies act as a beacon for investors, pointing out financing opportunities in sustainable sectors. According to the ECLAC (United Nations Economic Commission for Latin America and the Caribbean), "in 2022, $224.56 billion dollars of foreign direct investment (FDI) flowed into Latin America and the Caribbean, 55.2% higher than in 2021 and the highest since records began being kept" (2023). Due to green taxonomies, it will be possible to direct these investments towards renewable energy industries, clean transportation and sustainable management of natural resources among others, which make up part of the "dynamizing sectors of sustainable development". According to ECLAC:

> The adoption of taxonomies at the national level without proper coordination at a regional and/or global level may increase market fragmentation and generate competition problems, which will make it more difficult and expensive for participants in the financial market to understand

what a green or environmentally sustainable activity is. The financial sector is the most standardized sector at the global level and requires well-founded and harmonized standards on what can be recognized as a green or environmentally sustainable activity. In this vein, a set of comparable and interoperable definitions across jurisdictions would bring certainty, credibility, integrity and transparency to the market, facilitating the identification of investment opportunities for the private sector, specifically for domestic, regional and cross-border financial market participants and, at the same time, enabling the mobilization of private capital aligned to the goals of the Paris Agreement and other environmental policy objectives. (2022) [see figure 17]

Working well together will be essential, not only among each country's own agencies, but also between nations, so that the sum of efforts will in fact succeed in mitigating the consequences of climate change. Building this foundation is about common definitions for all, in such a way that investors have clear rules and standards.

For this reason, ECLAC indicates that:

The taxonomies of sustainable finance establish a common language and a definition, based on science, of "what is green or environmentally sustainable" and "what is not". The taxonomies of sustainable finance

FIGURE 17 / LATIN AMERICA AND THE CARIBBEAN: FOREIGN DIRECT INVESTMENT (FDI) RECEIVED

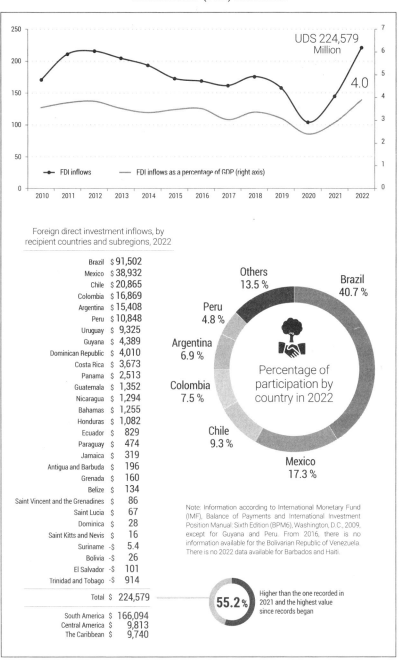

Foreign direct investment inflows, by recipient countries and subregions, 2022

Brazil	$ 91,502
Mexico	$ 38,932
Chile	$ 20,865
Colombia	$ 16,869
Argentina	$ 15,408
Peru	$ 10,848
Uruguay	$ 9,325
Guyana	$ 4,389
Dominican Republic	$ 4,010
Costa Rica	$ 3,673
Panama	$ 2,513
Guatemala	$ 1,352
Nicaragua	$ 1,294
Bahamas	$ 1,255
Honduras	$ 1,082
Ecuador	$ 829
Paraguay	$ 474
Jamaica	$ 319
Antigua and Barbuda	$ 196
Grenada	$ 160
Belize	$ 134
Saint Vincent and the Grenadines	$ 86
Saint Lucia	$ 67
Dominica	$ 28
Saint Kitts and Nevis	$ 16
Suriname	-$ 5.4
Bolivia	-$ 26
El Salvador	-$ 101
Trinidad and Tobago	-$ 914
Total	$ 224,579
South America	$ 166,094
Central America	$ 9,813
The Caribbean	$ 9,740

Percentage of participation by country in 2022

Others 13.5 %
Brazil 40.7 %
Peru 4.8 %
Argentina 6.9 %
Colombia 7.5 %
Chile 9.3 %
Mexico 17.3 %

Note: Information according to International Monetary Fund (IMF), Balance of Payments and International Investment Position Manual: Sixth Edition (BPM6), Washington, D.C., 2009, except for Guyana and Peru. From 2016, there is no information available for the Bolivarian Republic of Venezuela. There is no 2022 data available for Barbados and Haiti.

55.2% Higher than the one recorded in 2021 and the highest value since records began

SOURCE: ECONOMIC SURVEY OF LATIN AMERICA AND THE CARIBBEAN (2023). ECONOMIC COMMISSION FOR LATIN AMERICA AND THE CARIBBEAN (ECLAC).

– classification systems for environmentally sustainable activities – provide a clear guide to market participants on which activities are considered environmentally sustainable, in this way contributing to funnel investments that help boost the transition to a low emission and climate resilient economy. (2022)

Reduction of carbon emissions

Climate change requires drastic reductions in emissions. The green taxonomies, by highlighting climate friendly investments and practices, encourage the transition to a low carbon economy. According to the World Bank, investment in clean energy could reduce emissions in Latin America by 23% by 2030.

The EU "Taxonomy for Sustainable Activities" has been highlighted as an influential example. The European Commission estimates that, in order to achieve the objectives of the Paris Agreement, the additional investment needed in sustainable sectors could amount to 180 billion euros per year until 2030 (The Agora, 2020). Green taxonomy plays a key role in guiding this investment towards activities and projects that contribute to the transition towards a low carbon economy.

The energy sector is a key field for the implementation of green taxonomies. According to the International Energy Agency (IEA), the transition to renewable energy sources with CO_2 capture projects could reduce global emissions by 1.5 gigatons by 2030 (Global CCS Institute, 2020). The green taxonomies have the potential to further boost this process by providing clarity to the investors on the technologies and projects that are truly making progress towards climate goals.

Compliance with international agreements

Latin America has ratified the Paris Agreement and has set ambitious mitigation objectives. Green taxonomies provide a solid basis for measuring and reporting the progress, strengthening the regional position in global climate negotiations. According to the report by the Intergovernmental Panel on Climate Change (IPCC) in 2021, keeping global temperature increases below 1.5 °C requires a profound and rapid transformation in energy and economic systems. In this context, green taxonomies provide a solid structure for directing investments towards sectors and projects aligned with the climate objectives.

The taxonomy of the EU, for example, is directly linked to the Paris Agreement and seeks to ensure that investments are directed to sustainable economic activities. According to the report by the European Commission 'Sustainable Finance: Towards a Sustainable Growth', it is estimated that Europe needs to invest an additional €350 billion per year in sustainable activities in order to meet its climate and environmental objectives.

Promotion of technological innovation

Green taxonomies stimulate research and the development of clean and sustainable technologies in Latin America. By prioritizing investments in sectors aligned with environmental criteria, they encourage the creation and adoption of innovative solutions that will contribute to a more resource-efficient and low-emission economy. We cannot wait for environmentally responsible solutions to come from developed countries and then adopt them ourselves. In a globalized world, it is foolish to wait for innovations to come from abroad, when they can be carried out by local talent; talent that can work in tandem with their peers abroad to create authentic solutions that are tailored to our context.

Conservation and protection of ecosystems

Green taxonomies promote investment in the conservation and protection of the rich ecosystems of Latin America. By identifying and promoting projects and activities that preserve biodiversity and natural resources, the region's capacity to cope with the impacts of climate change is bolstered and long-term sustainability is ensured.

Colombia has been a pioneer in green taxonomies and has leveraged them as a crucial tool to address the challenges of climate change and move towards sustainable development. Our country, known for its rich biodiversity and varied ecosystems, has recognized the need to balance economic growth with environmental preservation. In this context, green taxonomies have begun to take shape as a guide for decision making and investment in key sectors.

Since their introduction in Colombia, green taxonomies have proved to have a positive impact on several fronts. First, they have catalyzed an increase in the investment in renewable energy and climate change mitigation projects. The clarity provided by green taxonomies has encouraged investors to back initiatives that reduce emissions and promote sustainability. This translates into more robust clean energy infrastructure and the diversification of energy sources, all aiming to reduce dependence on fossil fuels.

Colombia: a report on climate and development recently highlighted the country's leading role on this front:

In 2022, Colombia became the first country in the Western Hemisphere to adopt a national green taxonomy, in which the green assets and the green economic activities were identified and were classified and aligned with climate mitigation and adaptation objectives. This taxonomy will be used by all actors in the financial market: issuers of titles, investors, financial institutions, and entities of the public sector. In addition, the Colombian Financial Superintendence has incorporated elements related to climate action into the regulation of the sector (including disclosure and transparency requirements), developed tools to measure and monitor the risks related to climate change, regulated green financial instruments, and provided training. (International Finance Corporation, World Bank, 2023, pp. 16-17).

This report highlights how green taxonomies have led to the relevance of other similar exercises, but as a type of "blue taxonomy":

As an extension of the green taxonomy, the development of a blue taxonomy has become a priority, which will enable the private sector to play a prominent role in mobilizing funds for water related projects, such as protecting access to drinking water, wastewater treatment plants, recycling of plastics, restoration of marine ecosystems, sustainable river and maritime transport, ecotourism, and renewable energy in the high seas. (International Finance Corporation, World Bank, 2023, p. 17).

At the same time, green taxonomies have encouraged technological innovation in Colombia. The search for activities and projects aligned with environmental criteria has led to the creation of novel and efficient solutions to address local environmental problems. From the implementation of cleaner public transportation systems to the development of sustainable agricultural technologies, the focus on green taxonomies has stimulated the adoption of more climate friendly practices.

However, Colombia also faces difficulties and challenges in the effective implementation of green taxonomies. The lack of more accurate and complete data sometimes makes it difficult to identify and evaluate sustainable activities. The coordination among sectors and the training of key actors are also seen as challenges, as the understanding and application of green taxonomies require collaborative efforts and specialized knowledge.

In spite of these obstacles, Colombia is in a unique position to capitalize on the contributions of green taxonomies – and the blue taxonomy – to overcome the challenges ahead. By promoting transparency in decision-making and investment, the adaptation of clean technologies and the consolidation of inter-institutional efforts, the country can push forward on its path towards a more resilient and sustainable future.

5

30 × 30 Designation of protected areas

T he Strategic Plan for Biological Diversity 2011-
2020 was designed to address conservation and
the sustainable use of biological diversity around the
world. It was adopted in 2010 during the Convention
on Biological Diversity's (CBD) Conference of the Parties (COP), which is an international agreement that
strives to advance conservation and the sustainable use
of biodiversity. This strategic plan was undertaken
with the main objective of stopping the loss of biodiversity and promoting its sustainable use globally in
the 2010s. It is made up of twenty specific goals, known
as the "The Aichi Targets ", in honor of the Japanese city
where the plan was adopted. The plan approaches a
wide range of matters related to biodiversity, such as
the conservation of endangered species, the sustainable management of ecosystems, the mitigation of
threats such as the loss of habitats and the pollution

of the environment, as well as the promotion of public awareness of the importance of biodiversity.

This plan is also a key component of the United Nations Sustainable Development Goals (SDGs), in particular number 15, which focuses on life on land: "Life of terrestrial ecosystems: Protecting, restoring and promoting sustainable use of terrestrial ecosystems, managing forest sustainably, combatting desertification, halting and reversing the degradation of land, and halting the loss of biodiversity".

The plan has led to a series of initiatives and efforts at national and international levels to address the conservation of biodiversity and has been an important framework for global action in this area. The evaluation of its effectiveness and the development of a new framework for the period after 2020 was carried out in December 2022, during the United Nations COP15 Biodiversity Conference in Montreal, Canada, where it was agreed that the target to be pursued would be as follows:

Ensuring that, by 2030, at least 30% of continental waters and terrestrial, coastal and marine areas, especially areas of particular importance for biodiversity and their functions and ecosystem services, are conserved. Also, to make sure they are effectively managed through systems that protect and effectively conserve ecologically representative areas. These areas are to be connected and governed in an equitable way, recognizing the territories of indigenous and traditional peoples, all while ensuring that any sustainable use is fully consistent with conservation outcomes established, and recognizes and respects the rights of indigenous peoples and local communities, including their traditional territories. (Dudley & Stolton, 2022, p. iii)

Given that it holds the largest amount of environmental assets to conserve and its actions to mitigate the impact of the global warming are key, Latin America must take on the task of designating protected areas without omitting, of course, the very important participation of the native indigenous communities of each of these regions. Given the above, taking a census of its most precious treasure in order to protect it would be an important pursuit for Latin America. The signatory nations of the 2022 Montreal Summit Agreement reaffirmed their commitment to declaring 30% of their territories as protected areas by 2030. We know from experience in Colombia – where 34% of the territory has been declared as protected areas – that it is even possible to reach this percentage earlier, through a joint effort between governments, academia, communities and citizens. In Colombia´s case, we reached the goal eight years ahead of schedule.

Based on this, and on technologies that allow us to track and trace the activities that will be carried out in the territory, it will also be possible for conservation projects to become biodiversity credits, through which conservation is monetized via the capture of greenhouse gases. The idea is that these resources will be transferred to the communities who would otherwise be tempted to mine or grow crops illegally, cut down forests for livestock farming, agriculture and forestry, or carry out other types of activities that foster the illegal expansion of the frontier of arable land.

These protected areas are designated and managed for the purpose of preserving biodiversity, maintaining ecosystem services and mitigating climate change. Their contribution to preventing land degradation, uncontrolled urbanization and the loss of habitats is strategic. Characterized by their rich biological diversity, these areas often include key natural areas, critical ecosystems, and areas of cultural and spiritual importance. In Latin America, the natural riches and biodiversity are exceptional: it is home to a variety of ecosystems ranging from tropical rainforests to coastal deserts. Each country has to make its own type of designation, each country knows what it will need, each country knows which territories it has to protect; what is important is how to achieve a better understanding of protection capacity and how to certify it.

Protected areas play a critical role in the conservation of these ecosystems and the preservation of unique species: they have a fundamental place in the mitigation of climate change, as they contain vast carbon stocks and promote the resilience of ecosystems to climate impacts. They also have a direct impact on the fight against climate change, as many of these ecosystems store large amounts of carbon and act as crucial carbon sinks. Some examples of protected areas in Latin America include:

• *Sierra Nevada de Santa Marta National Natural Park, Colombia:* This protected area is home to a diversity of ecosystems, from tropical beaches to snowy mountain peaks. It is home to unique species and is considered an "island of biodiversity" due to its geographic isolation. Protecting the Sierra Nevada de Santa Marta is essential to preserving its biological richness and contributing to the mitigation of climate change by conserving forests and reducing carbon emissions.

• *Tambopata National Reserve, Peru:* In the Peruvian Amazon, this reserve protects a vast area of tropical rainforest. It features a great diversity of flora and fauna, including endangered species. Tambopata plays a vital role in the conservation of biodiversity and in capturing atmospheric carbon.

• *Canaima National Park, Venezuela:* This park is home to Roraima Mountain and a great variety of unique ecosystems. Conserving its habitats contributes to maintaining the integrity of its forests and helps mitigate climate change.

- *Nahuel Huapi National Park, Argentina:* Located in Patagonia, Nahuel Huapi is an example of South America's natural wealth. Its glaciers, forests and lakes are essential for the conservation of the biodiversity and climatic stability of the region. It is worth mentioning that several experts:

> [...] agree that sufficient natural or almost natural habitat remains for the 30 × 30 initiative (and the draft of the CBD Target 3) to be achievable, both on land and in the ocean. However, land areas continue to be lost and degraded at an accelerating rate, and such existing degradation implies that recovery will need to be added to the 30 × 30 target. Our study demonstrates that, under the right conditions, the target of 30 × 30 can be achieved without excessive cost, all while achieving a net benefit for the environment and society as a whole. (Dudley & Stolton, 2022, p. 3)

These protected and restoration areas, among others, are essential to counteracting global warming for a variety of reasons: by conserving biodiversity, ecosystems can remain resilient to climate disturbances; protected areas also act as carbon sinks by capturing large amounts of atmospheric CO_2 and reducing net emissions. The protection of coastal areas also helps to mitigate the impacts of rising sea levels.

These 30 x 30 protected areas not only preserve Latin America's unique biodiversity, but they also play a vital role in the worldwide fight against climate change. Through the conservation of these areas, we can ensure the sustainability of the ecosystems and contribute to the capture and storage of carbon, which at the same time will help mitigate the impacts of global warming. The successful implementation of this initiative requires a strong collaboration between governments, local communities and international organizations, with the goal of leaving a legacy of resilience and natural vitality for future generations.

The 30 × 30 initiative also has a positive impact on local communities and the indigenous villages who depend on natural resources. In fact, "the 30 × 30 target can only be achieved if the rights and territories of the Indigenous Peoples and Local Communities (IPLCs) are fully integrated" (Dudley & Stolton, 2022), as we will discuss further below. It is essential that any conservation plan includes a sustainable development perspective that respects the rights of these communities and encourages their active participation in the management of protected areas. In addition, this initiative can generate economic opportunities through sustainable tourism and scientific research.

The report *Best Practice in Delivering the 30x30 Target* also highlights that "There is strong evidence that this [the protection of 30 × 30 areas] will radically increase the success of the conservation of biodiversity. The success is measured in ecological, social, and economic terms, and ideally all three should be met at each site, or at least in the system as a whole" (Dudley & Stolton, 2022). In fact, the success of any environmental policy or restorative action needs to consider all three aspects, especially the human and community aspects, as is detailed in the same document:

> Successful conservation of an area takes advantage of diverse governance and management models and comes from the same people who use or live near the site, or is developed in collaboration with those people. In contrast, the methods used in the past have tended to be hierarchical and monolithic. While recognizing the enormous achievement of the compliance of the 11 Aichi Goals, we must rethink the approach for the 30 × 30 initiative and place greater emphasis on efficiency, ecological representation and human rights. An economic model must address seven issues:
>
> 1. *What to invest in:* State protected areas are the world's largest blocks of land and will continue to be very important, but there are alternatives emerging. There are many combinations of governance types and management approaches for protected areas, and the new category of "other measures of effective conservation by areas" (OMECs) adds many more. OMECs and indigenous peoples' and local communities' lands and territories (IPLCs) are examined in relation to their potential contributions to conservation.

2. *Where to invest:* Determining whether it is preferable for a country to improve the management of existing sites or add new areas, and in the latter case, where they should be located. The smaller, strategically located sites have been found to be more effective than larger, lower quality, and poorly managed sites that do not provide tangible results on the ground. They are offered as a decision tree and a guide on a series of data sources that can help chart a path to making smart decisions about the capacity needs and locations of the protected areas and OMECs.

3. *How to maximize the chances of success:* Decisions imposed from above and the forced displacement of people are not adequate responses to the biodiversity crisis. Initiatives from the ground up or grassroots processes are the strongest models for long-term success, which influences how time and money are spent, and which requires, at the same time, changes in donor policies, funding, monitoring and presentation of reports. We offer recommended steps for agreeing on a new protected area or OMEC and for improving existing protected areas.

4. *How to invest:* The financing of short-term projects runs the risk of creating infrastructures without the skills and resources to maintain them. We present different financing models, we analyze their strengths and weaknesses, and we offer a selection guide for a particular system.

5. *What else is needed:* Conservation by area is the cornerstone of success in the conservation of biodiversity, but it needs support, including sustainable management in the global setting, and supportive policies and laws. We lay out some key requirements.

6. *How to measure the benefits:* To convince the world to invest in the 30 × 30 initiative, it is necessary to have hard evidence showing that the benefits outweigh the costs. The protected areas and OMECs also provide many ecosystem services, so the costs are balanced against the benefits in terms of food and water security, disaster risk reduction and climate stabilization. We show how achieving the 30 × 30 target would be an impetus for many other targets of the GCBM, the Paris Agreement and many Sustainable Development Goals.

7. *Implementation on a larger scale:* Individual projects are not enough. There is a need for clear guidance on how to effectively apply the economic justification for area-based conservation over large areas of the land and ocean. (Dudley & Stolton, 2022)

In summary, the Strategic Plan for Biological Diversity 2011-2020, together with the global initiative to conserve 30% of terrestrial and marine areas by 2030, represent significant milestones in the fight for biodiversity conservation and climate change mitigation. Latin America, with its exceptional natural wealth and the crucial involvement of indigenous communities, is uniquely positioned to lead this historic effort. The designation of protected areas and the sustainable management of their environmental assets are essential steps to ensuring a resilient and sustainable future, in which conservation and productivity go hand in hand. We will go deeper into the protection of marine bodies in the following chapter and later, into the importance of local communities in the preservation, restoration, and environmental use of their territories.

6

Ocean and reef protection

The sea plays a key role in global temperature control because of its unique ability to absorb, store and release heat. For starters, the oceans act as heat sinks that absorb large amounts of the solar energy that reaches the surface of the Earth. This heat absorption is essential in moderating planetary temperatures and preventing its global temperature from rising out of natural control.

In addition to absorbing heat, the oceans also act as long-term thermal regulators. Seawater has a high heat capacity, which means that it can retain large amounts of heat without experiencing significant changes in temperature. This allows the oceans to store heat for long periods and release it gradually, which stabilizes the global temperature. This property dampens seasonal and regional temperature variations, thus providing a more balanced environment on Earth. However, such has been the magnitude of the heat absorbed that the temperature of the oceans and seas has risen, causing the poles to melt, sea levels to rise, coastal regions to erode (leading to a loss of marine territory on coasts and beaches), changes in the natural characteristics of the waters, and shifts in marine biodiversity and the livelihoods of communities living around it (see figure 18).

The oceans influence global weather patterns. Ocean circulation, such as the Gulf Stream, redistributes heat stored in the oceans around the world and thus affects regional and continental climates. For example, the Gulf Stream transports heat from the Gulf of Mexico to northern Europe, which moderates temperatures in that region.

Within the oceans there are coral reefs, which are extraordinary marine ecosystems that play a critical role in the health of the globe. In addition to their astonishing beauty and biodiversity, these fragile systems are essential for the mitigation of global warming and the preservation of marine biodiversity, as they are highly efficient carbon sinks, capable of capturing and storing large amounts of atmospheric CO_2. It is estimated that they cover less than 0.1% of the ocean floor but are home to about 25% of marine biodiversity. These ecosystems capture carbon through the process of calcification, in which corals build their skeletons using calcium carbonate. As CO_2 increases in the atmosphere, coral reefs play a crucial role in helping mitigate the impacts of climate change and reducing net carbon emissions.

Figure 18 / Effect of Climate Change on the Sea in Latin America and the Caribbean

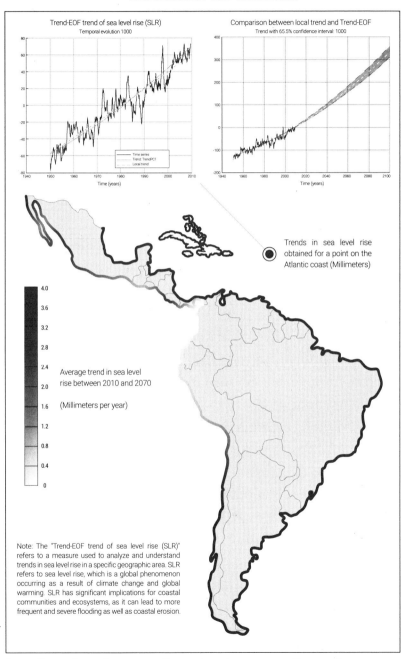

Source: Climate Change Effects on the Coast of Latin America and the Caribbean: Impacts - ECLAC (2012).

115

Coral reefs are home to extraordinary biological diversity. They are home to more than one million species, including fish, crustaceans, mollusks and other marine life. These ecosystems provide shelter, food and breeding grounds for many commercial and non-commercial marine species. In addition, the interconnection of reefs with other habitats, such as mangroves and seagrasses, amplifies their importance as nurseries and ecological corridors; this contributes to the health and resilience of marine ecosystems.

However, they face significant threats that endanger their existence and thus the stability of the oceans and the global climate balance. It is estimated that around 50% of the coral reefs in the world have already been degraded due to a combination of factors such as climate change, pollution, overfishing and coastal habitat destruction. Coral reefs around the world are critical to the livelihoods of 45% of marine species. Unfortunately, these marine ecosystems are under constant threat due to harmful practices such as trawling: an industrial fishing method that involves the use of high-capacity nets from boats that drag them across the seabed, catching everything in their path. The net has a front cavity that is kept open with the help of heavy doors or "crossbows" and, as it sweeps the seabed, it collects fish, crustaceans, mollusks and other organisms indiscriminately. Trawling is commonly used to catch commercial species such as shrimp, hake, cod and other bottom feeding fish, but in the process, it entangles others that have no commercial value and are often discarded. This method may be efficient in terms of catch, but it is also highly destructive to marine ecosystems. The action of dragging the net along the ocean floor destroys sensitive habitats such as coral reefs and seagrass beds.

When such a practice impacts a coral reef, its effect is equivalent to land-based deforestation, transforming biodiversity-rich habitats into vast marine deserts. Moreover, the continued degradation of these reefs and the resulting release of carbon dioxide is roughly equivalent to the annual emissions generated by the aerospace industry. Therefore, the protection of corals is imperative. Establishing protected areas and ensuring compliance is essential not only to preserving these ecosystems, but also to ensuring the sustainability of fisheries. Latin America has already taken significant steps in this direction, and it is crucial to continue advancing in this commitment. A report by the United Nations Environment Program (UNEP) warns that, if drastic measures are not taken, more than 90% of coral reefs could be in danger by 2050 due to global warming.

According to *The State of Biodiversity in Latin America and the Caribbean. An assessment of progress towards the Aichi Biodiversity Targets*:

In the marine realm, Caribbean coral reefs are diverse and globally important: 10% (26,000 km2) of the world's coral reefs are found in the western Atlantic Ocean, mostly in the Caribbean, and 90% of their species are endemic to the region. However, they are experiencing damage from rising sea temperatures and the combined effects of sediment runoff, introduced species, human population growth, land-based pollution, and destructive and unsustainable fishing practices. Changes in the health and distribution of coral reefs in the LAC region are most apparent in the Caribbean, where average coral cover declined from 34.8% in 1970 to 16.3% in 2011 at 88 sampling points, with the greatest changes overall occurring between 1984 and 1998. (UNEP & WCMC, 2016, p. 15)

Coral reefs are priceless natural treasures. Their role in climate change mitigation, biodiversity conservation and coastal protection is critical to the health of marine ecosystems and the sustainability of the planet as a whole. It is imperative for concerted global action to be taken in order to address the threats reefs are facing, including reducing greenhouse gas emissions, regulating fisheries, and implementing conservation practices. The preservation of coral reefs is not only for future generations, but also an investment in the resilience of marine ecosystems and global climate stability. In fact, they are ecosystems that can be regenerated relatively quickly and seeded to recover; nature once again showing its great resilience (Invemar, 2010).

According to *Best Practice in Delivering the 30x30 Target: Protected areas and other effective area-based conservation measures*:

> The management of marine areas for conservation has lagged far behind similar efforts on land. There are many reasons for this, including the status of marine areas beyond national jurisdictions as "common goods," the lack of visibility of marine species, the effectiveness and costs of monitoring and deeply held beliefs that the sea's resources are limitless. In particular, the relationship between the fishing industry and MPAs [Marine Protected Areas] has been strained. There is key evidence that strategically located MPAs lead to a net increase in fish in surrounding waters through surpluses, with no disadvantage to fisheries, as surplus individuals from protected spawning sites allow young fish to mature and maintain an older and much more fertile population. (Dudley & Stolton, 2022, p. 23).

An excellent example of a protected marine ecosystem is *La Amistad Regional Conservation Area*. It is a vast and significant area of approximately 401,000 hectares that encompasses parts of the province of Limón in Costa Rica and extends into the provinces of Bocas del Toro, Chiriquí and Veraguas in Panama. This area is known for its exceptional biodiversity, diverse ecosystems ranging from tropical forests and wetlands to high mountain *paramos* as well as for its role in the conservation of endangered endemic species. In addition to Costa Rica, Panama and Colombia, other Latin American countries have shown interest in participating in this trans-border conservation initiative, designated a UNESCO World Heritage Site since 1983.

La Amistad is not only a refuge for biodiversity, but it also has significant cultural value. Several indigenous groups, such as the Bribri, Naso and Ngäbe, have inhabited these lands for centuries and have maintained traditional natural resource management practices. These indigenous people have influenced conservation in the region and participated in the management of protected areas. However, human pressure, deforestation, agricultural expansion, natural resource extraction, illegal hunting, and other factors threaten the integrity of this protected area, unbalancing the environment and thus causing climate change.

If we succeed in designating at least 30 % of global marine areas as protected sites, we will ensure the preservation of marine life and the sustainability of the oceans. In addition, we will achieve a significant decrease in greenhouse gas emissions by safeguarding the cradle, the treasured habitat, of almost half of all marine species on our planet.

7

Green economies

The Industrial Revolution, which began in England in the 18th century and spread across the world, marked a turning point in the relationship between humankind and the environment. Increased mechanization and the use of fossil fuels such as coal and, later, petroleum, drove unprecedented economic growth, but also released massive quantities of carbon dioxide and other contaminating substances into the atmosphere. This change in the energy matrix was the start of an increase in emissions that would contribute to global warming and climate change.

As the 20th century rolled on, industrialization accelerated further with the expansion of production lines, capitalism and the unchained consumerism of the masses. The need for raw materials and their quick processing drove the extraction and trade of natural resources on a global scale. Soon, globalization would become the norm, pushing the intensive exploitation of forests, overuse of the oceans and the degradation of vital ecosystems. Furthermore, urbanization and the expansion of industrial agriculture have led to the loss of natural habitats and the extinction of numerous species.

The second half of the 20th century came with greater awareness of the consequences of these activities. Chemical experiments that affected the health of the population; the mercury contamination of entire bodies of water because there was absolutely no control; the accident at the Chernobyl nuclear plant (1986), that set off the terrible effects of acid rain across large parts of Europe and which the Soviet authorities tried to cover up; catastrophes out at sea, such as the Exxon Valdez (1989), Prestige (2002) and Deepwater Horizon (2010) oil spills; and international conflicts over oil in the Middle East that led to the deliberate dumping of oil in rivers and seas. These were all milestones in the continued damage to ecosystems and human life that eventually awakened public concern for the environment.

On top of all that, increasingly reliable scientific evidence that showed the effect of acid rain and the thinning of the ozone layer made it clear that the consequences of environmental damage affected every citizen in their daily lives. For example, the damage caused by household or personal aerosols to the atmosphere was evident, highlighting that pollution originated not only from large industries in the production phases but also from products that literally fell into the hands of citizens. Cars, to mention another example, became, as a result of their mass production and widespread use, sources of mobile pollution. All of this also initiated a movement showing that, if citizens had better information and awareness about the environment, they could make decisions about whether to use certain products. Free enterprise and market freedom offer the advantage that consumers have different product choices and can choose; the key is to educate these consumers about what to select based on ecological criteria.

All of this led to the creation of stricter environmental laws and regulations in many countries, and the signing of international agreements like the Montreal Protocol (1987), the United Nations Framework Convention on Climate Change (1992), the Kyoto Protocol (1997) and the Paris Accord (2015), with the aim of tackling climate change on the global stage.

Economic models have played a significant role in the creation of the current environmental crisis, given that they have historically been focused on economic growth at the expense of natural resources and sustainability. Traditional economic models were based on the idea of unlimited economic growth, where continuous production and consumption were the main objective. This often led to the over-exploitation of natural resources, environmental damage, and waste generation, without sufficient consideration for our planet's limits.

In many cases, economic models allowed companies to externalize environmental costs, meaning they did not bear the negative impacts of their production and activities on the environment; instead, they transferred them to suppliers or consumers, reducing direct costs and avoiding social or environmental responsibilities for their products. Nowadays, consumers are more informed and want to know the source of the raw materials used in the manufacturing of products (such as food, clothing, and even housing) and services (e.g., land or air transport, tourism services) and whether these comply with environmental certifications and sustainability protocols. Thanks to the internet, it is relatively easy for citizens to verify the accuracy of the information communicated by manufacturers with entities that monitor environmentally responsible processes. They can also express their dissatisfaction on social media when a company's "eco-friendly" promise does not align with reality. Today's consumers value the environmental reputation of companies more critically than they did ten or twenty years ago.

While this shift in consumer behavior is relatively recent, we cannot ignore the progress that our societies have achieved thanks to these economic models, which has been substantial. However, in the face of irreversible environmental damage, we are at a critical crossroads. Greenhouse gas emissions continue to rise, ecosystems are deteriorating, and the effects of climate change are becoming more evident and devastating. It is crucial for all public policies to include financial instruments and parameters that incentivize the transition to sustainable models, which not only avoid further harm to the environment but also contribute to decarbonizing it. Imposing carbon taxes has helped discourage environmentally harmful practices while encouraging innovation and transformation toward clean models. We cannot afford to stop production, much less slow down the economy by putting the brakes on its growth. As I have emphasized in various forums and writings, we need to produce while conserving and conserve while producing.

The environmental crisis is undeniable, but it also represents an opportunity to act. It is therefore time to make a transition towards models that adopt a circular economy approach, minimizing the extraction of natural resources and fostering reuse, recycling, the reduction of waste and the regeneration of products and materials. The aim of the circular economy is to maintain resources in use for the longest time possible and to reduce our dependence on finite natural resources:

• *Reduce:* This means reducing the quantity of waste that we generate in the first place. This can be achieved by purchasing long-lasting, quality products, through responsible consumption and awareness of the environmental impact of our consumer habits.

• *Reuse:* This is about using products or parts of products more than once before discarding them. This can involve repairing products, exchanging used goods, donating items we no longer need and any other way to extend the life cycle of products.

• *Recycle:* This refers to the process of collecting, processing and transforming materials in order to produce new products. Instead of throwing away materials like paper, plastic, glass and metal, these materials are gathered and turned into raw materials for new products.

A green economy makes up part of the same philosophy, but it focuses on investments and technologies that promote energy efficiency, renewable energy and the conservation of biodiversity (see figure 19).

This includes the creation of jobs in sectors such as green energy and the restoration of ecosystems. Economic models must incorporate a comprehensive evaluation of costs, considering the environmental and social impacts of economic activities. This means that companies should internalize environmental costs and pay for the natural resources that they use and the damage they cause, while the public sector must facilitate and promote this transition. This approach is totally different to the traditional approach taken in the 20th century. As the United Nations Development Programme stated in its report titled *Catalysing Climate Finance: A Guidebook on Policy and Financing Options to Support Green, Low-Emission and Climate-Resilient Development,* the premise is

To summarize, the economic models of the future should move away from the idea of unlimited growth and focus on environmental sustainability and responsibility. This implies a fundamental shift in the way we think of and manage our economy, with a focus on the conservation of natural resources and the promotion of human well-being on our planet. Sectors such as energy supply, transportation, construction, industry, agriculture, forestry, and waste management are critical for creating a green economy in our societies. "The existence of significant potential, with many options already available and cost-effective, should be argument enough for companies, private investors, and households to independently adopt priority mitigation and adaptation technologies," says Glemarec (2022, p. 18). He adds, however, that "investments in seemingly simple mitigation and adaptation technologies face a series of barriers." In this regard, public efforts should focus on reducing barriers to access a truly green economy, obstacles that include initially expensive investments that discourage entrepreneurs from opting for green models, high operating costs once implemented, unattractive tax incentives, a high price for the end consumer, limited availability of loans or unfavorable conditions, among others. Progress has been made on the path to a green economy, especially in developed economies, but there is still much to be done in Latin America.

Rather than a problem of capital generation, the key challenge of financing the transition toward a low-emission society is to address existing policy, institutional, technological, behavioral and technical skill barriers to redirect existing and planned capital flows from traditional high-carbon to low-emission climate-resilient investments. Removal of these barriers can complement and maximize the impact of capital finance such as concessional loan finance (Glemarec, 2011, p. 18).

So, when we talk about green economies, we need to understand that there are many important issues involved. One is everything to do with green financing, which relates to the issuance of green bonds as a mechanism to allow a nation to access the local and international market to secure capital allocated to investing in carbon neutrality and NDCs. In short, green bonds are those that a country or company offers in order to finance itself. To achieve this, having a green taxonomy is indispensable. Colombia was one of the first countries to issue green bonds, and several other countries have followed suit.

The green economy refers to an economic and developmental approach that seeks to improve human well-being and social equality while significantly reducing environmental risks and ecological scarcity. This definition is based on the report "Towards a Green

Economy: Pathways to Sustainable Development and Poverty Eradication," prepared by the United Nations Environment Programme (UNEP) (Herrán, 2012).

The components that make up the green economy include:

- *Efficient use of resources:* A focus on the efficient use of natural resources, the reduction of our carbon footprint and the optimization of the use of raw materials and energy.

- *Environmental conservation:* Promoting the conservation and restoration of ecosystems, biodiversity and the protection of critical natural resources like water and soil.

- *Renewable energy and clean technology:* Incentivizing the use of renewable energy sources, clean technology, and sustainable practices to reduce greenhouse gas emissions.

- *Employment and social equality:* Seeking to create green employment opportunities and promoting an equal distribution of social and economic benefits, with a special focus on the most vulnerable communities.

- *Innovation and sustainable development:* Promoting research and development for sustainable solutions, as well as the adoption of policies and regulations that promote sustainability.

• *Corporate responsibility:* Encouraging companies to adopt sustainable practices and to consider the environmental and social impacts of their operations.

• *Education and public awareness:* promoting environmental education and environmental awareness of the importance of sustainability and the protection of the environment.

The green economy is centered on the idea that economic growth and development can be compatible with the preservation of the environment and improving people's quality of life, if responsible and sustainable measures are taken. Once again, out of this environmental climate crisis we can forge a path of opportunities and hope.

The green economy, according to the previously provided definition, is intrinsically linked to the notion of carbon markets. These markets are a key component of the green economy, as they seek to deal with the problem of climate change by establishing an economic value for carbon emissions. They work as a mechanism that encourages businesses and countries to reduce their greenhouse gas emissions by allocating an emissions limit and allowing them to buy and sell carbon credits:

Carbon credits are a mechanism for pricing carbon. Each one represents one ton of greenhouse gases that has been reduced or removed through the development of a project or activity. The activity generating them must be carried out in accordance with established methodologies as part of Certification Programs (also known as standards). Thus, after the correct application of these methodologies contained in Certification Programs is validated and verified, it is understood that the reduction or removal can be credited, giving rise to carbon credits (De la Rosa, 2022).

This practice promotes resource efficiency by encouraging emission reduction and the adoption of cleaner technologies, aligning with the principles of the green economy. It is common for "carbon credits," also known as "offset credits" or "carbon offsets," to be confused with "green bonds." The latter refers to financial mechanisms issued to fund projects that provide both social and environmental benefits (De la Rosa, 2022).

In the context of the green economy, carbon markets play a crucial role in promoting investment in renewable energy and low-carbon technologies (see figure 20).

Companies that exceed their emissions limits can buy carbon credits from those that have managed to reduce their emissions below their allocated quotas, creating an economic incentive for the adoption of more

FIGURE 20 / CARBON MARKETS

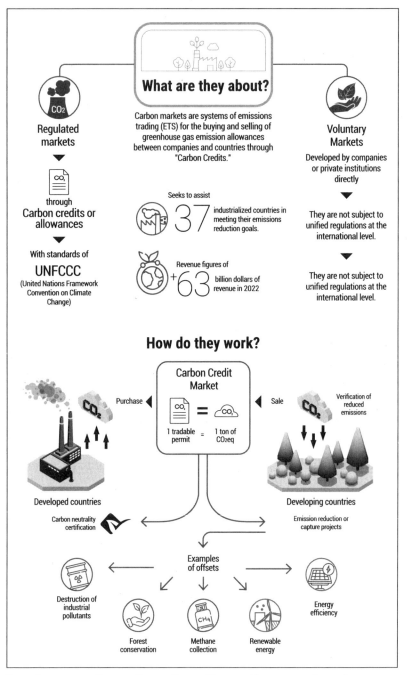

What are they about?

Regulated markets

Carbon markets are systems of emissions trading (ETS) for the buying and selling of greenhouse gas emission allowances between companies and countries through "Carbon Credits."

Voluntary Markets

through
Carbon credits or allowances

Seeks to assist
37 industrialized countries in meeting their emissions reduction goals.

Developed by companies or private institutions directly

They are not subject to unified regulations at the international level.

With standards of
UNFCCC
(United Nations Framework Convention on Climate Change)

Revenue figures of
+63 billion dollars of revenue in 2022

They are not subject to unified regulations at the international level.

How do they work?

Carbon Credit Market

Purchase ◄   1 tradable permit = 1 ton of CO_2eq ► Sale   Verification of reduced emissions

Developed countries

Developing countries

Carbon neutrality certification

Emission reduction or capture projects

Examples of offsets

Destruction of industrial pollutants

Forest conservation

Methane collection

Renewable energy

Energy efficiency

SOURCE: SELF-PREPARED - DATA FROM EMISSIONS TRADING WORLDWIDE / INTERNATIONAL CARBON ACTION PARTNERSHIP - REPORT (2023).

sustainable practices. This fosters the innovation and development of clean technologies, thus contributing to the green economy's objectives of reducing environmental risks and promoting human well-being.

Similarly, those who produce the most contamination must pay more taxes; this will disincentivize GHG emissions, as such emissions come with a consequence. As explained by the *Tax Policy for Inclusive Growth in Latin America and the Caribbean* document:

> Countries in Latin America and the Caribbean (LAC) could also increase their reliance on environmental taxes, which address a significant externality and contribute to mitigating the harmful effects of climate change. For example, carbon taxes are the most efficient instrument for reducing emissions and could generate additional revenue. Carbon taxes can also be useful in addressing the longstanding and pressing issue of high levels of informality in LAC, thereby increasing efficiency. As shown by Bento, Jacobsen, and Liu (2018), for instance, carbon taxes are difficult to evade in the informal sector and could enable governments to reduce the burden of other, more distortionary taxes that create a wedge between formal and informal activities (e.g., labor taxes). The combination of these elements, in turn, can lead to increased incentives for formalization, more efficient resource use, and, consequently, economic growth.

In Latin America, the green economy and carbon markets have gained traction over the last decade. Countries like Brazil, Mexico, Colombia, and Costa Rica have adopted policies and programs that promote the transition towards a more sustainable economy and are participating in international carbon markets.

There are currently: 1) direct taxes on carbon, 2) voluntary carbon markets and credits, and 3) regulated markets for carbon quotas and emission rights. Similarly, it is possible to report certain expenses incurred in the country as a temporary structural investment in climate action, which is not part of fiscal accounting, and can be represented as investments in social purposes or sovereign bonds, without impacting the debt indicator.

Among some benefits that the green economy and carbon markets can bring to the region, the following should be highlighted:

• *Sustainable economic growth and innovation*: The green economy can drive new economic sectors, such as renewable energy, and breathe new life into traditional ones, such as agriculture, by introducing and valuing techniques like agroecology, crucial for meeting global climate commitments.

• *Conservation of biodiversity*: Valuing ecosystem services promotes the conservation of natural areas and creates incentives for communities to be the primary custodians of environmental protection.

Green economy and carbon markets are promising approaches to addressing environmental and economic challenges in Latin America. Some examples of projects in the region leveraging these concepts include:

• *Sustainable Agriculture Program in Colombia*: This program promotes environmentally friendly agricultural practices and has benefited over 2,500 farming families.

• *Peninsula Wind Park in Mexico*: The wind park in the Yucatán Peninsula contributes to clean energy production and emission reduction.

• *Payment for Environmental Services in Costa Rica*: The country has implemented a program to pay landowners for the conservation of natural areas, as an incentive for natural resource protection.

• *Carbon Bonds in Brazil*: Forest and conservation projects in Brazil generate carbon credits sold in international markets.

• *Solar Energy Initiative in Chile*: Chile has experienced rapid growth in solar energy generation, diversifying its energy matrix and reducing emissions.

As the region continues to seek more sustainable and resilient development, the implementation of practices and policies based on these concepts can generate significant benefits for biodiversity, the mitigation of climate change and the welfare of communities (see figure 21). Nevertheless, overcoming obstacles and intersectoral collaboration will be essential for achieving a successful transition to a greener, low-carbon economy in the region.

There are individuals, nations, or companies that, with the aim of reducing their carbon footprint, buy these credits and can thus claim to offset the damage caused by their emissions through conservation projects. This capture of CO_2 tons that a country or private project carries out on behalf of another is certified. Similarly, regions willing to reap these benefits can offer their environmental capacity to sell green bonds. For example, in Colombia, in the department of Caquetá, there has been an analysis of how to transform the entire Amazon area into green bonds, which would bring in around 45 billion pesos [$11.5 million USD] annually if these policies were implemented. A recent report by the consulting firm Deloitte states:

> The need for carbon markets in Latin America lies in the opportunities, benefits, and challenges they pose as new ways to fulfill corporate commitments, as well as an increase in demand for these markets worldwide. One of the key components for harnessing carbon markets is the

FIGURE 21 / CARBON MARKETS IN LATIN AMERICA AND THE CARIBBEAN

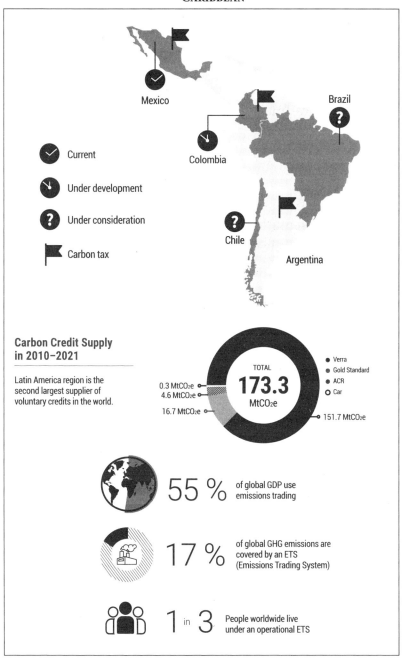

SOURCE: EMISSIONS TRADING WORLDWIDE / INTERNATIONAL CARBON ACTION PARTNERSHIP - REPORT (2023).

sources of financing available in the region. Development financial institutions such as the IDB or the World Bank allocate significant resources to the development of institutional capacities in relevant issues, in addition to scaling up private investments in low-carbon and resilient initiatives. (2022, p. 7)

Latin America has experienced significant growth in voluntary carbon markets in recent decades, with numerous successful initiatives contributing to climate change mitigation and sustainable development in the region. Some successful experiences in Latin America include:

• *REDD+ Program in Acre, Brazil:* The state of Acre in Brazil has implemented a successful Reducing Emissions from Deforestation and Forest Degradation (REDD+) program. Through this program, Acre has successfully reduced deforestation, preserved its extensive forest areas, and sold voluntary carbon credits on the international market. This initiative has demonstrated that forest conservation can be profitable and has improved the living conditions of local communities.

• *Peace Forests, Colombia*: The "Peace Forests" initiative in Colombia focuses on forest conservation and the promotion of peace in areas affected by armed conflicts. Voluntary carbon projects in these areas have contributed to carbon emission reductions while improving security and stability in local communities.

• *Quilapilún Solar Plant, Chile*: Chile has been a leader in adopting renewable energy, and the Quilapilún solar plant is a standout example. This solar facility generates clean energy and sells carbon credits in voluntary markets, helping fund additional solar and wind energy projects in the country.

• *Cordillera Azul Project, Peru*: This forest conservation project in the Cordillera Azul region of Peru has protected an area of tropical rainforest the size of Rhode Island, reducing carbon emissions and preserving biodiversity. The generated carbon credits have been purchased by sustainability-committed companies and governments.

• *Carbon Footprint, Mexico*: Mexico has seen an increase in the adoption of corporate carbon footprint programs, where companies voluntarily calculate and offset their carbon emissions. This approach has led to the development of renewable energy and reforestation projects, contributing to the transition to a low-carbon economy.

These are just a few examples of successful voluntary carbon market initiatives in Latin America. These projects not only help reduce greenhouse gas emissions, but they also have a positive impact on local communities, biodiversity conservation, and sustainable development throughout the region. The path is a promising one, and we must continue to explore it.

8

Debt-for-climate swaps and voluntary carbon markets

Multilateral debt-for-climate swaps refer to the provision of financial resources by international and multilateral organizations to developing countries. The aim is to alleviate the burden of their external debt, allowing them to invest in projects and programs addressing the impacts of climate change and promoting environmental sustainability. Generally, countries in the region have high levels of indebtedness and have issued sovereign debt bonds related to environmental and climate goals. Once the bond is placed on the market, the country benefits from reduced interest rates, a discount known as a "green premium," contingent on meeting the agreed-upon criteria.

These funds are allocated to activities ranging from adaptation and mitigation to the promotion of clean energy, the conservation of ecosystems and the improvement of climate resilience. According to the International Monetary Fund:

Debt swaps for climate and nature action aim to release fiscal resources, allowing governments to enhance resilience without triggering a fiscal crisis or sacrificing spending on other development priorities. Creditors offer debt relief in exchange for the government's commitment, for instance, to decarbonize the economy, invest in climate-resilient infrastructure, or protect the biodiversity of forests or reefs (Georgieva et al., 2022).

In this regard, the most relevant organism in the world is the Green Climate Fund (GCF). The GCF has provided funding to 228 projects in more than one hundred countries, aimed at reducing deforestation, promoting sustainable agricultural practices, and improving the resilience of local communities. "Its mandate is to foster a paradigm change towards development paths that are low in carbon emissions and resilient to climate change in developing countries", and therein lies its vital importance in processes of clean transportation, among others (Inter-American Development Bank [IADB], 2022).

By alleviating the burden of debt, it is possible to reallocate financial resources to projects aimed at sustainability and resilience. Yet, despite their benefits, multilateral debt-for-climate swaps also face some challenges. The identification and evaluation of suitable projects, transparency in the use of funds and the effective coordination between governments and multilateral organisms are all key aspects to be considered. In fact, a large part of mitigating the impact of global warming requires constant investments that are properly directed at key sectors, such as energy transformation. According to the *Catalysing Climate Finance* report by the United Nations Development Programme (UNDP):

> Achieving this transformation will require a dramatic shift in public and private investments from traditional energy supply sources and technologies to more sustainable climate-friendly alternatives. The International Energy Agency (IEA) estimates that the capital required to meet projected energy demand through 2030 in a non-carbon constrained world would amount to $1.1 trillion per year on average. Approximately half of this will be required for developing countries, roughly evenly distributed between the large emerging economies (China, India, Brazil, etc.) and all remaining developing countries. Additional investment of close to $10.5 trillion ($510 billion per year over the next 20 years) over a business-as-usual fossil fuel scenario is needed globally in the energy sector for the period 2010-2030 to ensure a 50 percent chance of maintaining GHG concentration to less than 450 ppm CO_2e (IEA, 2009). (Glemarec, 2011, p. 10)

It is clear to see that the greatest levels of GHG contamination have been produced by countries that have historically enjoyed the most industrial development; the large economic powerhouses are the sources of the greatest environmental damage. Their energy-intensive economic activities, such as industrial production and transport, have released huge quantities of carbon dioxide (CO_2) and other contaminants into the atmosphere, which has contributed to the increase in global temperatures and extreme weather events. However, they are also the countries with the biggest head start in terms of ecosystem recovery, the implementation of clean technology and the creation of stricter legal frameworks in their territories in order to mitigate CO_2 emissions. But their job does not end there, and they cannot lay the responsibility for creating solutions and facing the responsibility on Latin America alone.

An August 2022 report by the International Monetary Fund states:

> Debt swaps have been part of the debt restructuring landscape since the Latin American debt crisis. The first debt swaps include a tripartite swap in 1987 with Bolivia led by Conservation International and a bilateral swap in 1989 between the Netherlands and Costa Rica. Since then, over 100 debt swap operations have been carried out: at least 50 tripartite swaps and approximately 90 bilateral debt swaps involving around 15 official creditors (in some cases, more than one at a time) and benefiting about 30 debtor countries. These include 10 transactions between

the United States and Latin American debtor countries under the 1990 Enterprise for the Americas Initiative and around 20 transactions under the U.S. Tropical Forest Conservation Act of 1998 (Chamon et al., 2022).

The path taken by these countries serves as an example for developing nations, so that they do not repeat mistakes and begin, as quickly as possible, to replace, for example, the use of hydrocarbons for transportation, encourage companies to follow high standards of clean production, and raise awareness among citizens about environmental care. Latin America has the opportunity not to repeat the mistakes of other countries. However, being countries with fewer resources, they require mechanisms to finance their transition towards "a green, low-emission, and climate-resilient development" (Glemarec, 2011, p. 62).

The United Nations Framework Convention on Climate Change (UNFCCC), capital markets, multilateral and bilateral agencies, government agencies, and private organizations have created favorable environments for financing projects and initiatives with a clear path in the green economy. "More than 90% of climate financing comes from private markets (venture capital, asset financing, etc.). However, public financing is essential to remove barriers to climate technologies and to attract direct investments," explains the report (see figure 22).

FIGURE 22 / CLIMATE FINANCING

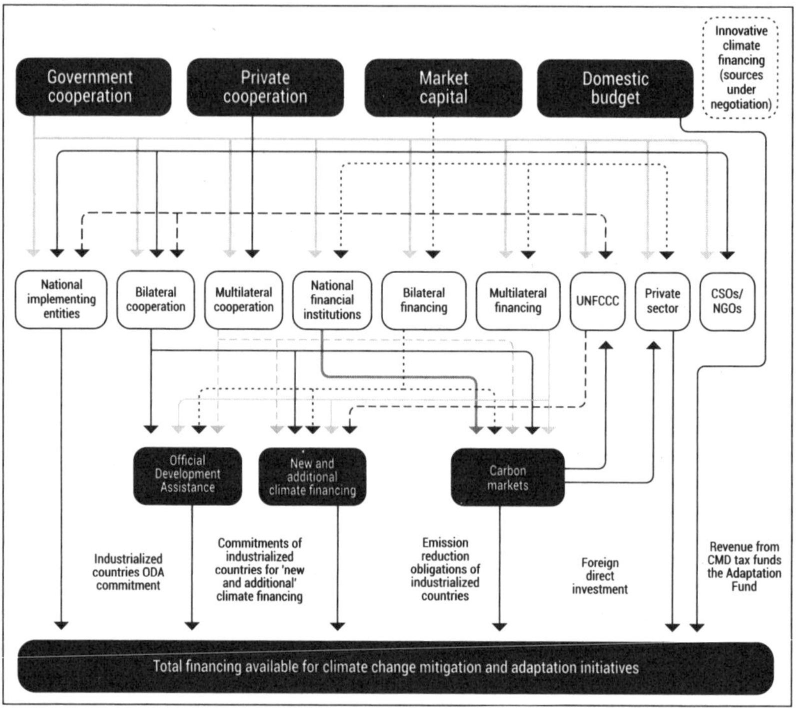

SOURCE: ADAPTED FROM GLEMAREC (2011).

In the context of green economies, multilateral financing of debt for climate action is an essential element. Similarly, voluntary carbon markets play an important role in this equation; these markets allow companies and countries to offset their carbon emissions by investing in emission reduction projects in other regions. This investment can be an additional source of financing for climate action in developing countries since carbon mitigation projects can generate income through the sale of carbon credits in these markets. This, in turn, can strengthen the green economy by incentivizing the implementation of clean and sustainable technologies.

The combination of multilateral financing of debt for climate action and participation in voluntary carbon markets can generate a constant flow of financial resources towards projects and policies promoting sustainable development and adaptation to climate change. This can drive economic growth and improve the quality of life of vulnerable communities.

All of the above is part of the Clean Development Mechanism (CDM), which is a set of provisions established in 1997 in the Kyoto Protocol. Its objective is to assist industrialized countries in meeting their greenhouse gas emission reduction targets by promoting mitigation projects in developing countries.

The CDM allows industrialized countries to fulfill part of their emission reduction commitments by investing in emission reduction projects in developing countries, such as those in Latin America. These projects may involve improvements in energy efficiency, the implementation of renewable energy, and the capture of greenhouse gases. Once established, they generate Certified Emission Reductions (CERs), each equivalent to one ton of carbon dioxide whose emission has been avoided or reduced. These credits can be used by industrialized countries to meet their emission reduction targets or they can be sold on the international market.

9

Energy transition and the green hydrogen path

Reducing the greenhouse gas emissions that cause global warming requires plenty of innovation, research and creativity. Much of the technology we use today was created to make use of hydrocarbons and other carbon derivatives. Our daily life still runs on hydrocarbons; the energy transition, that is replacing carbon and petrol with other energy sources such as gas, solar, wind or electric, requires a significant effort, both in terms of money and time.

The energy transition is a process of fundamental change in the way we produce, distribute and consume energy, driven largely by the need to tackle climate change and progress towards a more sustainable future. Throughout history, we have experienced many important milestones that have shaped this transition, which is taking place at different speeds around the world. It is important to note that this is a gradual transition that does not necessarily imply totally replacing some energy sources overnight, rather it involves reducing the demand for certain sources in order to make way for others that involve fewer or zero GHG. As Bill Gates states, it is also possible to "shift the load" or "shift the demand" through a more coherent use of energy, which involves changing habits, routines, and schedules.

At the start of the Industrial Revolution, towards the end of the 18th century and the beginning of the 19th century, the use of coal became extensive, marking the dawn of the era of fossil fuels. Then, at the end of the 19th century, vast petrol reserves were discovered, leading to an even greater reliance on hydrocarbons. However, the petrol crisis in the 1970s highlighted the vulnerability of petrol-based economies and pointed to the need to diversify our energy sources. Furthermore, despite the destructive power of nuclear energy being starkly demonstrated by the bombs dropped by the United States on Hiroshima and Nagasaki, European powers started nuclear energy projects in order to meet the internal demand for energy, until the devastating incident at Chernobyl showed how dangerous this was.

As a response, renewable energies, such as solar and wind, began to gain prominence in the 1990s. Technological advancements and policies supporting these energies worked to drive their growth, making them increasingly competitive with respect to fossil fuels. In 2015, the Paris Accord established the objective of limiting global warming to below two degrees centigrade, which requires a mass transition to low-carbon energy sources.

From an economic perspective, investment in renewable energy has increased significantly, reducing the costs of solar and wind energy and creating employment in sectors such as solar panel installation and wind farm construction. In the long term, this transition could lead to a reduction in costs and more stability in terms of energy prices.

In terms of sustainability and the environment, the energy transition seeks to drastically reduce carbon emissions, which is essential to halting climate change. It can also contribute to reducing pressure on natural ecosystems related to the extraction of fossil fuels. Furthermore, it promotes cleaner and more sustainable energy sources, such as solar and wind, which reduces the environmental degradation associated with the extraction of fossil fuels.

In this context, it is essential to look at the technologies being implemented today. For example, theories of greenhouse gas capture are being developed, even in the hydrocarbon sector. There are methods to capture CO_2 and reinject it into the ground. Additionally, artificial intelligence technologies are being used to monitor protected areas, carry out reforestation programs, and combat deforestation. Advances have also been made in irrigation technologies. It is important to highlight the predominant technologies in the sector and how they are contributing to the reduction of greenhouse gas emissions.

The timeline of innovations in green energy reflects the constant progress towards the energy transition we have been witnessing over the last few decades. Between the 1950s, when the first solar panels were developed, and today, we have seen advancements in the materials and the technology that make them more affordable and effective. At the same time, the technology for generating wind power has also become more efficient and reliable since the 1980s, with the creation of larger wind turbines and the optimization of their design. Many regions of Europe are dotted with enormous turbines that, with their huge blades, loom like giants over the landscape. These contribute to the 255 GW of wind capacity in the Old World. In 2022, 19 GW of new wind capacity was installed, a 4% increase compared to 2021. The question that arises is why we haven't been able to successfully replicate this model throughout Latin America.

One of the challenges of renewable energies, particularly electricity, is their intermittency. However, in recent decades, we have seen advances in storage technologies, such as lithium-ion batteries, which allow for the storage of energy generated by intermittent sources like the sun and wind for use later on. In his book, Bill Gates points out:

[...] we are going to need much more clean electricity in that near future. Most experts agree that, as other emission-generating processes, such as steel manufacturing and vehicle circulation, electrify, the global electricity supply will have to double or even triple by 2050. And this doesn't even take into account population growth or the fact that people's quality of life will improve, leading to increased electricity consumption. Consequently, the world will need much more than triple the electricity we generate today.

Furthermore, the digitalization and automation of electricity networks has allowed for more efficient and flexible management of energy through intelligent networks.

Sustainable transport, which I will talk about in more detail later, has seen significant advancements in electric vehicles, with the improvement of batteries and the expansion of the charging infrastructure. Additionally, geothermal and biomass energy have also seen technological advancements, with increasingly efficient and accessible geothermal systems and a more sustainable approach to the use of biomass as an energy source.

Recently, green hydrogen, produced through electrolysis with renewable energy, has piqued interest as a clean and versatile energy source. Meanwhile, innovations in energy efficiency in buildings, industries, and transportation have contributed to reducing energy demand. Additionally, as we address carbon emissions, carbon capture and storage (CCS) technologies are advancing to decrease emissions from existing sources.

It is vital to understand that energy transition is not a question of ideology. Despite the existence of opinions, often without much economic or technical basis, that advocate for the complete elimination of petrol and gas without putting forward a consistent transition plan, these energy sources continue to be valuable resources that generate royalties for the public finances of many nations, and which are difficult to replace at scale. Shutting down these sources abruptly would be counterproductive, as we need a planned transition to avoid a loss of income and the disruption of our ability to move towards more sustainable technologies. We need legal approaches and fiscal incentives for the development of cleaner energies and their integration into electrical grids.

So, increasing the installed capacity of wind and solar energy, and harnessing surpluses, can provide us with the opportunity to produce green hydrogen on a large scale. Latin America should look to become a leader in green hydrogen production over the next decade. Not only do we have the capacity to produce from renewable sources, thanks to regions with wind speeds higher than those in northern Denmark, but we also have a large solar capacity due to constant sunshine in many areas.

Green hydrogen is undoubtedly a boost towards energy sustainability in Latin America. Green hydrogen has emerged as a promising alternative in the quest for sustainable solutions to global energy and environmental challenges. This form of hydrogen, produced from renewable energy sources, presents itself as a path towards the decarbonization of key sectors of the economy. Green hydrogen, also known as renewable hydrogen, is produced through water electrolysis using renewable energy such as solar or wind power. Unlike gray hydrogen, which is produced from fossil fuels, green hydrogen does not emit carbon during its production or use. The benefits of green hydrogen are varied, ranging from reducing greenhouse gas emissions to diversifying the energy matrix and creating employment in related sectors. The production process of green hydrogen involves the separation of hydrogen and oxygen from water through electrolysis. The resulting hydrogen is stored and can be used as fuel in vehicles, industry, or even in electricity generation through fuel cells. In October 2022, María Fernanda Suárez Londoño, former Minister of Mines and Energy of Colombia, wrote in a column published in the Latin America edition of El País:

> When there is an energy source that is reliable, non-polluting, and reasonably priced, oil and gas will come to an end. If they persist, it's not because of a conspiracy but because new technologies have not yet competed with them in providing reliable energy at reasonable prices. That's why the emphasis should be on the world investing

in science and technology with the vigor, speed, and determination it had to develop vaccines for Covid-19. There are three critical technologies that, if they become commercially viable and affordable for consumers, will accelerate the transition: large-scale storage (batteries for energy generated by renewable sources), carbon capture and storage (to continue using hydrocarbons without releasing the carbon they produce), and hydrogen. Meanwhile, giving up on developing current energy sources amounts to shooting oneself in the head. (Suárez Londoño, 2022)

Although she wrote this with the case of Colombia in mind, it is equally fitting for the rest of the continent. Latin America has huge potential to produce green hydrogen, thanks to its abundance of renewable resources. Chile, with its solar radiation and strong winds, has the profile to be a leader in the production of green hydrogen. Argentina and Uruguay also possess significant wind and solar resources, giving them an advantage when it comes to developing this emerging industry:

Several countries in Latin America and the Caribbean have expressed interest in producing green or blue hydrogen or ammonia to meet the anticipated demand for low-carbon fuels. Chile and Brazil are estimated to have one of the most competitive potentials for green hydrogen production globally, while Panama is well-positioned to meet the new demand for low-carbon fuels in the maritime sector. (World Bank, 2022, p. 18)

Meanwhile, in the Andean region of Latin America, Colombia stands out as a country actively exploring green hydrogen production. The Colombian government has announced plans to develop a green hydrogen roadmap with the aim of driving the transition to a low-carbon economy. Conversations have been initiated with various sectors to promote research and development projects and encourage investment in technologies related to green hydrogen. Although the initial costs of green hydrogen production can be high, they are expected to decrease as technology develops and expands. However, there is still a long way to go to make it as inexpensive as producing energy with hydrocarbons.

10

Green transportation

G reen transportation, also known as clean transportation, has become an unavoidable necessity in our current context, which is characterized by climate change and growing urbanization. Latin America, amidst its rapid urban growth and the challenges posed by traffic congestion and atmospheric contamination, faces a reality in which transforming transport systems is a pressing issue.

Despite some progress in the adoption of electric vehicles and the development of infrastructure for bicycles and public transport, the region still depends largely on fossil fuels in the transport sector. This situation can be seen in cities like Mexico City, Sao Paulo, and Bogota, where congestion and contamination are daily problems that affect the quality of life of residents.

The World Health Organization (WHO) has identified several Latin American cities amongst the most polluted in the world in terms of fine inhalable particles

(PM 2.5), which are damaging to our health; Mexico City, Lima and Bogota are among the most affected.

Green transportation has the power to revolutionize the way that people get around and consume. According to figures collected by the Inter-American Development Bank (IADB), the adoption of electric vehicles in Latin America is on the rise, with an increase of 60% in sales between 2020 and 2021. Furthermore, the promotion of efficient and sustainable public transport alternatives can influence transport choices. The rise in ride sharing services and microtransit solutions, and increased use of bicycles and electric scooters, are redefining the experience of moving around cities.

The transition towards green transport can potentially have a significant impact on the quality of life of citizens. A reduction of congestion and improvement of air quality can translate into a 30% reduction in greenhouse gas emissions related to transport in cities. According to the United Nations Environment Programme (UNEP), the adoption of efficient public transport systems could reduce CO_2 emissions in Latin American cities by up to 37%. Additionally, encouraging the use of active means of transport, such as walking and riding bicycles, can lead to healthier lifestyles, which in turn will contribute to a reduction in silent, chronic diseases in the population.

From a climate perspective, green transport plays a crucial role in the fight against climate change. The Inter-American Development Bank (IADB) has pointed out that approximately 20% of greenhouse gas emissions in the region come from the transportation sector. The adoption of electric vehicles and the transition to cleaner fuels can significantly reduce these emissions and contribute to greenhouse gas reduction goals in line with international agreements.

Despite its potential, green transport faces considerable challenges in Latin America. According to data from the World Economic Forum, the high initial costs of acquiring electric vehicles, a lack of charging infrastructure, and necessary cultural shifts are obstacles that must be overcome. However, these difficulties also represent opportunities for technological innovation, investment in infrastructure, improved connectivity at work locations in urban centers, and collaboration between the public and private sectors.

Green transport can radically transform Latin America by changing how people move, consume, and live in their cities. The region faces the challenges of urbanization due to the proportion of its population looking to move away from traditional urban centers. This context gives rise to new cities and new opportunities for growth with proper planning and consideration of the issues raised by the climate crisis.

The COVID-19 pandemic highlighted the opportunity to change transport habits for citizens. As people had to stay at home during extended quarantines, the possibility of studying and working from home became evident. Receiving goods and products through urban delivery networks or using alternative means of transportation such as bicycles or scooter – some electric due to gasoline shortages – or simply walking in cities became more common. This realization also highlighted the fact that living in the most populous urban centers was no longer essential, and living in new, less dense, and more affordable places was viable while maintaining the same economic activities.

Post-COVID-19 mobility in Latin America, especially in cities like Bogotá, Buenos Aires, Mexico City, Sao Paulo, and Santiago de Chile, underwent ten substantial modifications, as outlined in the report published by ECLAC (United Nations Economic Commission for Latin America and the Caribbean) titled *The impact of COVID-19 on transport mode preferences in selected cities in Latin America:*

- Macro trends in transport and immobility
- Changes in the public transportation system
- Changes in individual transport strategies
- Motorcycle boom
- The impact of deliveries
- Road safety
- Limited increase in cycling infrastructure
- Expansion of public spaces and increased demand for recreational spaces
- Relocation of people, businesses, and services
- Telecommunications factor

This list, according to the researchers, "does not aim to be exhaustive or definitive, but to reflect the phenomena identified during or as a result of the pandemic that are most relevant to urban mobility." Perhaps it was one of the positive effects of that terrible event because it made us aware that there were other ways of doing things, not just theoretically or as an isolated case, but as something practical and of massive scope.

According to the *Roadmap for Climate Action in Latin America and the Caribbean 2021-25*, transport in Latin America requires urgent modifications to reverse the trend that has been followed for decades of using gasoline vehicles:

> To decarbonize passenger transport, the growing motorization rate must be curbed by investing in cleaner modes. These also deliver productivity-enhancing co-benefits, such as improved accessibility and the reduction of congestion, pollution, and road accidents. E-mobility programs are gaining momentum in most countries in LAC, resulting in the development of charging station corridors in 11 countries and electric bus systems in 13 countries. Incentives for e-mobility as well as emissions reduction in the trucking industry (which transports nearly 75 percent of domestic freight in LAC) include the reduction of fossil fuel subsides, tighter emissions standards, and fleet renewal programs. Such measures can also boost innovation and support regional transformation, for example by

stimulating manufacturing of electric buses and trucks through the greening of transport fleets. In countries that import fossil fuels, decarbonizing the energy system and transport will improve the balance of payments and reduce currency risks associated with fossil fuel price volatility. Moving away from fossil fuels will also reduce the scale of and demand for fuel subsidies, releasing resources to fund social programs in line with long-term development goals. (World Bank, 2022).

The same document also states:

Enabling safe nonmotorized mobility has substantial emissions reduction potential, especially when combined with policies to disincentivize the use of motorized vehicles. Moving people from their private cars and motorcycles to nonmotorized modes such as walking or biking can save up to 62 percent of life cycle GHG emissions for each trip. Successful initiatives include the large investment in biking infrastructure in Bogota that led to an 8 percent increase in the biking modal share. Such investments can be combined with "push" measures, including the definition of low-emission zones, congestion pricing and parking management. In Mexico City, Bogota, and Santiago de Chile, congestion pricing, resulted in a reduction of motorized travel of up to 29 percent. 15 A Roadmap for Climate Action in Latin America and the Caribbean

Additional WBG support for low carbon urban design and the decarbonization of urban mobility is an urgent priority to avoid the lock-in of carbon-intensive urban forms in Argentina, Bolivia, Brazil, Colombia, Ecuador, Haiti, Mexico, and Peru, some of the countries with the largest urban populations in the region. (World Bank, 2022).

The pandemic also revealed the profound environmental damage caused by air travel. When forced to avoid travel, we witnessed the possibility of holding remote, virtual events, even massive entertainment events. Of course, nothing replaces a live performance by our favorite artists or the staging of certain events; however, the virtual option created new markets, new ways of consuming events, and other ways of coming together to learn and work. Above all, for the latter, we saw the enormous potential of virtual working dynamics. Studying for a degree virtually is now possible and accepted; as for jobs, we have already mentioned that it is perfectly viable for many professionals to offer their services remotely or from home. Offices sat empty and, since the pandemic, have remained partially occupied as hybrid work schemes emerged, where employees are only required to go to the office occasionally. On a larger scale, business trips were also limited to those that were strictly necessary during the pandemic and only by essential personnel, which has now become the norm. The aviation industry was one of the major casualties during the pandemic, perhaps the hardest blow it has received since September 11, 2001.

In environmental terms, pollution from air travel decreased; therefore, this trend is favorable and highly desirable. Airlines were forced to modify their environmental protocols as well, all of which helps mitigate the negative impact that travel has on the environment. On this topic, the report *Climate Change and Development in Latin America and the Caribbean Overview* states:

> The mitigation of CO_2 emissions in the aviation sector in the medium term depends on increasing fuel consumption efficiency through improvements in design technology for aircraft and engines and better air traffic operation and management. These gains may only partially offset the increase in emissions from this sector, however. (CEPAL, 2009, p. 117)

We will not stop moving about, but thanks to innovation and technology, we can do it in a smarter and more environmentally friendly way.

11

Low carbon agriculture and sustainable livestock management

There are a series of crucial issues, ranging from the implementation of silvopastoral and agroforestry systems to the adoption of more efficient irrigation systems. It is essential to foster more awareness around how agricultural products are used and managed, from planting to harvesting. We need to focus on minimizing our carbon footprint throughout the agricultural process. In this regard, we can see some successful strategies employed in countries including Brazil and Guyana, who have implemented measures to reduce the environmental impact of agriculture. It is fundamental that we highlight regional examples that can serve as an inspiration and guide for other countries in the region.

One of the most noteworthy actions is the adoption of silvopastoral practices, which involve a reduction in the areas allocated for livestock and a greater rotation of grazing land. This approach not only improves productivity, but it also contributes to a healthier diet for the livestock, which in turn has a positive impact on the emission of greenhouse gases. Silvopastoral systems have the capacity to capture CO_2, which makes them a valuable tool in the fight against climate change. Another crucial aspect relates to water management; innovations in irrigation systems can make a significant difference in terms of efficiency and the reduction of waste.

An inspiring example can be seen in La Fazenda, located in the Meta department of Colombia, where they have tackled the issue of methane, a harmful greenhouse gas emitted by livestock. By capturing this gas, La Fazenda has not only managed to mitigate its environmental impact, but also to generate electricity from the captured methane. These initiatives show that agriculture can be an active player in finding climate solutions, integrating sustainability and the generation of green energy.

Ultimately, the conversation about sustainable and low-carbon agriculture encompasses a range of innovative approaches that go beyond simple food production. The combination of practices such as silvopasture, water management, and greenhouse gas capture, along with concrete success stories in different regions, represents a crucial step towards more resilient agriculture that is aligned with climate change mitigation goals. Agriculture and livestock play a key role in the economy and food security of Latin America, but they also significantly contribute to greenhouse gas (GHG) emissions and global warming. Faced with this challenge, the search for innovative and sustainable solutions has given rise to concepts such as "low-carbon agriculture" and "sustainable livestock management." These strategies represent a paradigm shift in agricultural and livestock production, aiming at reducing carbon emissions and promoting resilience to climate impacts.

Low-carbon agriculture seeks to minimize the carbon footprint of agricultural systems by reducing greenhouse gas emissions and maximizing carbon capture. This is achieved through more efficient agricultural practices, optimizing the use of materials, and adopting soil management techniques that conserve and improve soil health. According to the FAO, agriculture in Latin America contributes approximately 15% to global greenhouse gas emissions, underscoring the urgent need to adopt low-carbon approaches.

Scientific investigations have shown that practices such as conservation agriculture, agroforestry and crop rotation can significantly reduce carbon emissions. A study published in *Nature Climate Change* highlighted the fact that the adoption of agroforestry systems in Latin America could reduce carbon emissions by up to 50% compared with conventional systems.

Sustainable livestock management focuses on balancing livestock production with the conservation of natural resources and the mitigation of greenhouse gas emissions. The goal is to improve efficiency in meat and milk production, reduce the environmental impact of livestock farming, and ensure animal welfare. Latin America is one of the regions with the highest levels of livestock production globally, but it also faces challenges related to deforestation and the emission of greenhouse gases associated with this activity.

The implementation of practices such as sustainable intensification, improved animal feed, and waste management in livestock farming can reduce emissions of methane and nitrous oxide, two potent greenhouse gases (GHGs). Studies indicate that the application of manure management techniques in beef production systems in Latin America could potentially decrease methane emissions by up to 40%.

The adoption of low-carbon agricultural practices and sustainable livestock management can have a significant impact on the fight against climate change and global warming. According to the World Bank, the implementation of sustainable practices in agriculture and livestock could reduce greenhouse gas emissions in Latin America by up to 37% by 2030.

According to the *Roadmap for climate action in Latin America and the Caribbean 2021-2025*:

A distinctive feature of greenhouse gas (GHG) emissions in Latin America and the Caribbean is the large share from agriculture, and land-use change and forestry, which together account for 47 percent of emissions across the region, significantly exceeding the global shares of these sectors (19 percent of global GHG emissions). (World Bank, 2022)

Despite the progress and potential benefits, the widespread adoption of low-carbon agricultural practices and sustainable livestock management faces challenges such as a lack of financial incentives, resistance to change, and the need for training. This highlights the importance of strengthening green markets. However, it also presents opportunities to improve productivity, resilience, and food security in the region. Climate-smart agriculture will be essential in two senses: on the one hand, in terms of cultivating fields with a view to the conservation and preservation of water resources and the health of the land itself, including its mineral characteristics; on the other hand, in meeting the growing demand for food through productive activity. For this task, it is crucial to prevent the expansion of the agricultural frontier, by avoiding deforestation at all costs, as well as to make the most of the land designated for cultivation.

The United Nations Food and Agriculture Organization (FAO) defines agricultural and farming systems as sustainable if they meet the needs of current and future generations, while also guaranteeing profitability, the protection of the environment and social and economic equality. Sustainable agriculture and food systems follow five fundamental principles: 1) increasing productivity, employment and added value in food systems; 2) protecting and strengthening natural resources; 3) improving subsistence means and fostering inclusive economic growth; 4) strengthening the resilience of people, communities, and ecosystems; 5) adjusting government management to new challenges. Sustainable, low carbon agriculture provides benefits for both adaptation and mitigation. It contributes to mitigation by reducing greenhouse gas emissions from agricultural and livestock practices and supports adaptation by minimizing negative effects such as groundwater pollution, soil conservation, and deforestation. (PAHO & WHO, 2018)

The *desertification* of our soil represents some of the greatest damage committed by human beings on the planet. Agriculture has been one of our species' age-old practices in order to provide us with sustenance. In the 1940s and 1950s, as a result of the world wars, much progress was made in terms of industrializing agriculture, with the aim of producing more food in less time, but not a thought was given to the deep, long-term impact this would have on the erosion of soil and destruction of ecosystems.

The earth, our soil, is fertile if it maintains the balance between the microorganisms living in it and the minerals. Soil itself is rich, which is why it produces food. It is rich in carbon, and carbon per se is not harmful; CO_2, however, is detrimental to human health. The carbon cycle is a fundamental natural process that involves the constant movement and transformation of carbon on Earth. Carbon exists in different forms in the atmosphere, biosphere, lithosphere, and hydrosphere. We are made up of carbon particles and other elements: oxygen (65%), carbon (18%), hydrogen (10%), nitrogen (3%), calcium (2%), phosphorus (1%), and in smaller amounts, elements like potassium, sulfur, sodium, chlorine, magnesium, iodine, iron, and zinc. The problem arises when there is an excess of carbon dioxide in the atmosphere, for which plants provide us with a tremendous service. Let's briefly review the carbon cycle:

• *CO_2 Emissions:* The CO_2 cycle begins with the release of carbon dioxide into the atmosphere. This occurs through natural processes such as plant and animal respiration, the decomposition of organic matter, volcanic activity, as well as the burning of fossil fuels through human activities.

• *CO_2 Absorption:* Plants, in particular, play a fundamental role in this cycle. Through the process of photosynthesis, plants absorb atmospheric CO_2 using solar energy.

• *Photosynthesis:* Photosynthesis is a chemical process through which plants, in the presence of sunlight, absorb CO_2 and release oxygen (O_2), while they convert the CO_2 into glucose and other organic molecules. This conversion of carbon dioxide into organic matter is essential to the production of food and energy in the food chain.

• *Carbon Storage:* Plants store carbon in the form of biomass, and this carbon is transferred to herbivores when they consume plants. Carnivores then obtain carbon by consuming herbivores as part of the food chain.

• *Respiration:* Both plants and animals undergo cellular respiration, the opposite process to photosynthesis, in which CO_2 is released as a byproduct when glucose is broken down to obtain energy. This returns CO_2 to the atmosphere.

• *Transfer to the Food Chain:* Through the food chain, carbon is transferred from one organism to another as consumers gain energy and carbon by consuming other organisms.

• *Decomposition:* When organisms die, their remains are decomposed by bacteria and fungi. During decomposition, CO_2 is released into the environment as organic compounds break down.

• *Fossils and Fossil Fuels:* Some carbon is stored long-term in the lithosphere, forming deposits of organic carbon such as peat, lignite, oil, and coal. Over geological time, pressure and heat transform these deposits into fossil fuels. Burning these fuels releases CO_2 into the atmosphere.

• *Carbon in the Oceans:* Atmospheric CO_2 dissolves in seawater, where it can be used by marine photosynthetic organisms. Additionally, oceans store large amounts of carbon in the form of calcium carbonate, found in the skeletons of marine organisms.

This carbon cycle is essential for maintaining the climate's balance and life on Earth. However, human activities such as the burning of fossil fuels and deforestation have disrupted this cycle by releasing large amounts of CO_2 into the atmosphere, contributing to climate change.

The soil plays a fundamental role in all of this. Excessive plowing has turned fertile soil into deserts, transforming nutrient-rich land into useless dust. This over-plowing has converted large expanses of soil into fields for experimentation and the use of enormous amounts of chemically derived fertilizers to make the land productive again. This supposed solution turned out to be worse than the problem, depleting the soil's nutrient potential and permeating it with substances that are poisonous for humans, which have leaked into bodies of water and been transmitted into our food.

Soil desertification is a concerning phenomenon affecting many regions worldwide, with the progressive degradation of fertile land in dry and semi-arid areas. This process is primarily caused by natural factors such as lack of precipitation and climate variability, but also by unsustainable human activities like deforestation, intensive agriculture, excessive grazing, and uncontrolled urbanization.

One of the most notable effects of desertification is the loss of land productivity, leading to a decrease in the ability to support plant and animal life and the degradation of local ecosystems. Furthermore, desertification has severe social and economic consequences, as it can trigger the forced migration of communities dependent on the land for their subsistence, exacerbating poverty and food insecurity.

Today, less harmful agricultural practices have been developed that do not plow the soil but instead create spaces for planting seeds and allowing water to enter and hydrate the soil. Plowed soil loses its natural consistency, preventing water absorption and causing runoff, leading to avalanches and mudslides.

There is another side to this: livestock farming. By destroying the soil and rendering it infertile, there are no pastures for livestock to graze on. Therefore, chemical nutrients must be created for the animals because their natural food source no longer exists. Grazing livestock no longer roam free; they are confined to feedlots or limited areas. The significant impact of cow and ruminant emissions as air pollutants, particularly CO_2, is well-known.

The connection between cow dung and climate change is linked to the production of methane, a potent greenhouse gas. Cows, like other grazing ruminants, have a specialized digestive system that involves microbial fermentation in their stomachs to break down the fibrous plant foods they consume. Methane is produced as a byproduct during this fermentation process and is primarily released through cow flatulence and burps, and to a lesser extent, through their dung.

Methane is a greenhouse gas with a much higher global warming potential than carbon dioxide (CO_2). Despite being present in much smaller quantities in the atmosphere compared to CO_2, its heat-trapping capacity is considerable and significantly contributes to climate change. Feeding livestock with non-natural substances further increases these emissions.

As it's not feasible to eliminate the livestock industry entirely, it is essential to develop methods that help reduce this negative impact. Similarly, a return to productive yet natural agriculture is crucial. This is possible if we understand that soil is not an infinite resource but something that must be managed intelligently to avoid depletion. Ancient cultures managed this with their ancestral knowledge, and today, we have advanced technologies to curb soil misuse and reverse its effects. Nature consistently demonstrates its regenerative and resilient power.

Family solutions, households making a difference, the circular economy

We have repeatedly spoken about the importance of individual commitment when counteracting the effects of climate change. We have also stressed that we cannot lay all the responsibility on government or state actions. It is time for each one of us to accept our starring role in this universal act. It sounds grandiose, but it really isn't; the size and scale of the catastrophe that we are silently living through merits the emphasis. Every citizen of the world can contribute, in their own way, to reducing their carbon footprint, reducing their consumption of single-use plastics and materials, and reducing their consumption of fossil fuels for transport.

Let's consider an average household. There are a number of actions that each member can take for the environment, to contribute to less contamination and helping those outside the household who are dealing with much weightier tasks. There is no one-stop list of actions; each household should evaluate its own habits and adjust its routines accordingly in order to make them more environmentally friendly. Climate change has been the result of a chain of actions coming from the use and sustained abuse of natural resources by human beings. Reversing this pattern, or at least slowing its accelerated growth, can also be the result of a chain of preventative actions that promote the efficient use of resources and respect for our life source, planet Earth.

This is where it is not about figures or policies, but about common sense. It is not about governments or policymakers, but about conscientious citizens. I urge you to analyze the details of your household. How do you deal with trash? What products do you buy? How do you use electric energy or water resources? What options do you look to for your household's transport needs?

To reduce our carbon footprint in our homes, we can start by implementing energy-saving measures. It is important to replace incandescent lightbulbs with energy-efficient LED bulbs and disconnect electronic devices when we are not using them. Additionally, we should opt for efficient appliances with an A++ or higher rating to decrease our energy consumption. Choosing efficient appliances, such as highly energy-efficient washing machines and dryers, as well as refrigerators and freezers with inverter technology, can significantly contribute to reducing energy consumption.

We should consider generating renewable energy by installing solar panels on our roofs; this will make us less dependent on the conventional electrical grid and decrease our carbon emissions.

To reduce water wastage, it is essential to repair leaks in faucets, toilets, and pipes. Moreover, we can install low-flow showerheads and faucets to decrease water consumption in our homes. We should also be rational with the length of our showers.

Ensuring that our homes are well-insulated and sealed to prevent heat or cold escaping will help us to be more efficient with our central heating and air conditioning. Using programmable thermostats to adjust the temperature based on the time of day and our homes' needs is also an effective measure.

In terms of transport, we should consider using bicycles or public transport instead of private vehicles. If possible, we should invest in electric vehicles (bicycles, motorbikes, and scooters, for example, as well as cars, of course) or hybrid options to reduce greenhouse gas emissions.

It's also important to adopt the principle of reducing, reusing and recycling. We must minimize waste by buying products with less packaging and choosing reusable products instead of disposable options. Before we print a document, we should stop and think about whether we really need to. Be sure to separate and recycle materials according to the local guidelines that exist in most cities or municipalities. If there are none, follow standards that can easily be found online.

Let's try to foster conscientious consumption by choosing local, seasonal products in order to reduce the carbon footprint associated with the transport of foodstuffs. It is also important to reduce our consumption of meat and other animal by-products, given that meat production has a major environmental impact.

In our gardens, let's opt for native plants that require less water and fertilizers; speaking of which, we should avoid using chemicals and seek alternatives made from natural products. Let's compost organic waste to reduce waste and enrich the soil; there are local organizations that can provide guidance on the disposal of this by-product. Education and awareness are key. Let's educate our families about the importance of reducing our carbon footprint and promote sustainable practices in our homes. Finally, let's support clean energy and sustainable policies by participating in community initiatives related to sustainability and endorsing policies that promote clean energy and the reduction of carbon emissions. Indifference is an ally of global warming and a key factor in its increased effects.

In rural areas, practices or customs that have been adopted in some homes due to a lack of resources or information should also be eliminated. Traditional houses have wood-burning stoves for food preparation. This practice is still common but not advisable. One way to replace this is clean cooking, which refers to the use of clean technologies and fuels for cooking, with the aim of improving people's health and quality of life and protecting the environment in regions where biomass burning (wood, dung, charcoal, etc.) is still used on open or rudimentary stoves. These rustic systems produce a large amount of smoke and harmful particles that people inhale during cooking, leading to respiratory issues, chronic lung diseases, and other health problems, especially in women and children who tend to spend more time in the kitchen. The term clean cooking is directly related to replacing traditional cooking methods, such as biomass burning on open or rudimentary stoves, with clean and efficient options. In Latin America, these methods are still used and are sources of high contamination and greenhouse gas emissions, in addition to promoting deforestation.

Clean cooking solutions include the use of renovated stoves and kitchens that utilize cleaner and more efficient fuels such as liquefied petroleum gas (LPG), biogas, ethanol, and electricity.

In Colombia, traditional methods have been replaced with solar panel-based solutions for individual households. These solutions are particularly suitable for dispersed and isolated communities lacking access to the conventional electrical grid. For example, in municipalities like Crucito in Córdoba, Taraira in Vaupés, and others near Mavecure in Guainía, such solar panels have been successfully implemented, providing a reliable energy source for cooking, and enhancing the safety and quality of life of local communities.

Just as indifference is an ally of global warming, consumerism has also played a role. This refers to a pattern of people acquiring and consuming goods and resources in excessive quantities, often beyond their basic needs. This behavior, driven by a culture of accumulation and materialism, has a significant impact on climate change.

Firstly, consumerism leads to an increase in the demand for manufactured products, resulting in higher levels of industrial production. This production often relies heavily on fossil fuels, such as oil and natural gas, for energy and transportation, leading to a massive release of greenhouse gases into the atmosphere.

Secondly, the life cycle of consumer products, from manufacturing to disposal, also contributes to climate change. The extraction of natural resources, production, transportation, and waste management generate carbon emissions at each stage. Moreover, many consumer products are made with petroleum-based plastics, exacerbating environmental pollution and the plastic waste crisis.

Finally, consumerism encourages a "use and discard" mentality, increasing the amount of waste and garbage generated. Improper waste management, including landfills and incineration, contributes to the release of greenhouse gases and other pollutants into the atmosphere and soil. Moreover, consumerism can deplete natural resources, such as wood and water, in an unsustainable fashion, further exacerbating environmental issues.

As an antidote to this, the circular economy has proven to be an attractive alternative, initially championed by young people, although it has gained more followers and practitioners. The circular economy is an economic and business approach that seeks to change how we produce, consume, and manage resources, with the goal of reducing waste and minimizing environmental impact. Instead of following the linear model of "take, make, use, and discard" that is the basis for traditional economies, the circular economy is based on principles of sustainability and efficiency. The main components of the circular economy include:

- *Sustainable design*: In this approach, products are designed with their entire life cycle in mind from the outset. This involves selecting durable materials, increasing ease of disassembly and recycling, and waste minimization.

- *Reuse*: Rather than discarding products at the end of their lifespan, reuse is encouraged. This can involve repairing and restoring products to extend their lifespan or renting and exchanging products instead of purchasing.

• *Recycling and material recovery*: The recycling of materials and the recovery of resources from products at the end of their lifespan are promoted. Recycled materials are used to create new products, thus closing the cycle.

• *Zero waste*: Efforts are made to minimize waste generation as much as possible. This includes proper waste management and the adoption of practices that minimize waste production in the first place.

• *Renewable energy and energy efficiency*: The circular economy also covers the issue of energy by promoting the use of renewable energy sources and improving energy efficiency in all sectors.

• *Sustainable business models*: Business models that focus on offering services rather than products are encouraged.

The circular economy aims to reduce the pressure on natural resources, minimize waste generation, and decrease environmental pollution. This approach is crucial for addressing contemporary environmental and economic challenges, such as climate change, scarcity of resources, and waste management. It can also generate economic opportunities by driving innovation, efficiency, and job creation in sustainability-related sectors.

13

Biodivercities

The climate crisis can be seen more acutely in the cities, given the increased intensity of activities such as construction, transport and waste management. Therefore, it is fundamental to generate a collective conscience in urban areas, where any action taken by a city, its government entities, utility companies and, of course, its citizens should incorporate the protection of biodiversity, not simply as one of its fundamental objectives, but as the main one. Cities are the meeting point for natural and human ecosystems.

To exemplify this connection between ecosystems, it is essential to highlight the case of Bogotá, a city standing at 2,600 meters above sea level that depends on the biodiversity of the Sumapaz, Cruz Verde, Verjón, and Piedras de Moyas *paramos* (high Andean ecosystems, unique to Colombia, Ecuador and Venezuela) to supply its water. Despite their importance as veritable "water factories," the *paramos* are under pressure due to human activity, jeopardizing their role in regulating the water cycle and potentially having broader impacts, even as far as in the Amazon. These *paramo* ecosystems are intrinsically linked to the Amazon and play a crucial role in water regulation and the conservation of endemic species such as the *frailejon*, a unique plant species with enormous environmental value. However, the sustainability of these ecological connections largely depends on how cities manage their resources. If cities consume water and energy irresponsibly and do not effectively address air quality and waste management, they will jeopardize their own sources of livelihood. Given Colombia's rich biodiversity, it is essential for urban residents to understand how their behaviors can directly impact this heritage. The responsibility lies in adopting consumption habits that are conscious of and respectful towards biodiversity.

Latin America needs its cities to continue expanding but under a framework of respect for the environment and life; hence, I refer to them as "biodivercities." These are new cities that educate their citizens in environmental care and provide them with the tools to do so through policies and clear communication about what they can and cannot do; such education must start in schools, universities, businesses, and all organizations, led by the cities.

Latin American cities have a peculiarity: their lack of planning and unchecked growth, a phenomenon that has defined them for a long time, but which has experienced accelerated growth in recent decades. These urbanization processes have been driven by a combination of factors, including population growth, rural-to-urban migration, and industrialization. In countries like Colombia, this has been exacerbated by the historical displacement of populations during the many stages of violence our country has endured. Cities have overflowed. There have been regulations, zoning plans, reforms, and public urban planning measures, but they have been insufficient to meet the demand for space brought about by human migration. The deep damage caused by corruption is also not insignificant, allowing uncontrolled urbanization; this has often led to catastrophes arising from not assessing natural risks in constructions in geologically unstable areas or near water sources, or in programs for the management of the tons of daily waste produced by a city that are either inadequate or underscored by private interests.

The reality is that the trend towards urban growth shows no signs of stopping. Construction is increasing, cities are becoming more densely populated, road infrastructure is more and more insufficient, and the number of private vehicles increases each year. This leads to hours of congestion, contributing to increased pollution. Similarly, public service offerings and infrastructure fall short in the face of demographic growth. All over the world, this has triggered migration towards smaller urban centers or municipalities on the outskirts of major cities, which are starting to experience the same pressures, as they were not prepared to accommodate more people. The possibilities and advantages demonstrated by remote working, allowing tasks and work functions to be performed without being in an office, have facilitated this decentralization once again.

As a result, many growing cities in Latin America face significant challenges related to urban planning, the provision of basic services, affordable housing, and urban transport. This rapid urban expansion has led, on the one hand, to the proliferation of informal settlements as well as formal neighborhoods within already established cities. On the other hand, it has led to the development of new urban or industrial hubs in smaller cities or those previously considered "bedroom cities" – urban areas near a major city where most residents work in the major city but choose to live in the bedroom city due to proximity and quality of life. These have become places where remote work is possible thanks to connectivity.

Urban changes will always exert pressure on natural resources; this is inevitable. The challenge lies in minimizing this pressure and planning the migration processes toward these new urban centers in an environmentally friendly and sustainable manner. The climate crisis, therefore, can be critically seen in cities, where inadequate infrastructure for waste management, limited implementation of waste-to-energy technologies, and air pollution caused by burning fossil fuels are triggering adverse consequences. The absence of effective systems to reduce, recycle, and reuse materials, as well as wasteful water consumption, jeopardizes air quality and the environment.

In this context, technology plays a crucial role by providing tools to measure and track greenhouse gas emissions in urban environments. Additionally, technology can empower citizens to set individual goals as "biodivercitizens" and take concrete actions to reduce their own emissions. Ultimately, the transformation towards sustainable and biodiversity-friendly cities requires collective commitment backed by tangible technologies and measures.

Today, it is impossible to consider the economic, social, and environmental development of a city separately from its transportation systems. These systems have always defined the character of cities and their citizens in terms of social behavior and efficiency of movement. Cities like Curitiba in Brazil, and Bogotá or Medellín in Colombia, have made progress in this regard by creating multimodal systems that include mass transit buses, increasingly powered by electric motors and less by diesel or gas, cable cars, subways, trams, and public bicycle systems and bike lanes.

Additionally, the use of LED lighting on streets, charged during the day with solar panels, is another significant advancement. Public regulations that require official buildings to turn off lights during non-working hours also contribute significantly to reducing the energy consumption of cities.

It is crucial to support people who recycle with training, by organizing them into work cooperatives, and ensuring fair income for their work. Their work is essential in utilizing reusable solid waste in cities, a task that will never be complete without waste separation at the source. European countries are decades ahead in this awareness; the United States and Canada have also been doing this for many years. In contrast, in Latin America, it is still not a common practice for all households, from Patagonia to the Rio Grande, to separate waste at the source. But even if we did, if every step of the cycle is not followed, it will be of little or no use.

What would we gain by separating waste at the source if garbage collection continues to be done in the same way, and it all ends up mixed again?

Where the private sphere ends, the public must begin to operate to fulfill the purpose. Although there is already legislation in many cities and countries on these processes, there is still a long way to go. For example, single-use plastics or materials like expanded polystyrene (known in Colombia as "*icopor*"), a non-degradable material still used to pack food or, paradoxically, in school or university tasks, should be banned. It makes no sense for children in schools to be asked to make a model of the Solar System and paint Styrofoam spheres, including one representing planet Earth in blue and green tones. Just as with polystyrene, we must avoid, regulate, or understand the proper disposal of materials such as:

• *Conventional plastics*: Most plastics, such as polyethylene, polypropylene, PVC, and PET, are highly resistant to biodegradation and can persist in the environment for centuries.

• *Aluminum*: Aluminum is a metal that does not naturally biodegrade. While it is recyclable, the extraction and manufacturing process is energy intensive.

• *Glass*: Glass is another material that does not biodegrade. Although highly recyclable, it can remain in the environment for an extended period if not properly recycled.

• *Heavy metals*: Metals like lead, mercury, and cadmium are toxic and non-biodegradable. Their release into the environment can have serious health and ecosystem consequences.

• *Nylon*: This is a synthetic material used in textiles and other products. It is known for its durability and resistance to biodegradation.

• *Synthetic chemicals*: Many human-made chemicals, such as certain pesticides, paints, dyes, detergents, and industrial chemicals, are non-biodegradable and can be harmful to the environment if released.

The lack of biodegradability of these materials means that they will accumulate in the environment if not managed properly through recycling, reusing, or responsible disposal. Authorities in every large or small city, town, or municipality must ensure that their residents know how to recycle, reuse, and reduce their consumption of these materials; without information, citizens are unlikely to comply with regulations. The approach should be educational rather than punitive, but in the case of any violations, it is necessary to enforce appropriate sanctions that set precedents for both individuals and businesses.

14

Green entrepreneurship

W e have already mentioned the essential role that the public sector has to play in mitigating the impacts of climate change and global warming. Using public policies, governments should establish frameworks within which the private sector and citizens in general can act. Through measures such as the protection of property rights, the promotion of favorable business environments and fair regulations, governments can create favorable conditions for individuals to start businesses and effectively develop their ideas. These policies must encourage investment, innovation, and competition, at the same time as guaranteeing legal protection and equal opportunities.

This is how governments can not only stimulate economic growth but also empower citizens to pursue their entrepreneurial aspirations, producing benefits for both individuals and society as a whole. In this context, mitigating the effects of climate change is not solely the responsibility of the public sector, which provides a framework for action, but also that of the private sector, regardless of its size.

In *Our Future*, we all need to take action – public entities, private businesses, groups, individuals; every person on Earth should have a vision for protecting the environment and making appropriate use of natural resources. It is crucial for the government to ensure that the private sector has the necessary elements to develop its initiatives, and that these initiatives align with the green economy. The state needs private initiative; it cannot suppress the private sector overnight or stifle it to the point where, out of weariness, entrepreneurs prefer to take their capital out of Latin American countries.

By "entrepreneur," I refer to anyone wanting to start a business – offering goods or services, investing capital, and expecting a return on that investment – regardless of the business's size, market sector, or the stage of development. Whether in the initial phases of exploring and incubating new businesses (entrepreneur) or in the more established phase of managing a business (businessperson), both play crucial roles.

Private entrepreneurs and businesspeople should not be seen as enemies of the state or the public sector. Rather they should be considered essential partners in economic and social development, as well as in the fight against climate change. In a mixed economy, interaction between the private and public sectors is fundamental for progression. Private entrepreneurs and businesspeople provide investment, generate employment and drive innovation, contributing to economic growth. That is why they can play a crucial role in the transition towards a more sustainable economy. The state, for its part, has the responsibility to regulate and supervise – with clear and fair rules – business activities, in order to guarantee or protect public interest and promote responsible environmental policies. Similarly, supervision and regulation are not enemies of private initiatives. The state must guarantee fair play and freedom of competition in just conditions, such that it acts as a protective instrument for entrepreneurs and businesspeople. When they work together, the private and public sectors can create a balance that benefits society as a whole, through the promotion of welfare, economic growth and, above all, the mitigation of climate change. This is one of the most pressing challenges of our time, if not the most. It is worth highlighting what is mentioned in the report "Climate Change 2022: Impacts, Adaptation, and Vulnerability:"

> Investment in social and technological innovation could generate the knowledge and entrepreneurship needed to catalyze system transitions and their transfer. The implementation of policies that incentivize the deployment of low-carbon technologies and practices within specific sectors, such as energy, buildings and agriculture, could accelerate greenhouse gas mitigation and deployment of

climate resilient infrastructure in both urban and rural areas. Civic engagement is an important element of building societal consensus and reducing barriers to action on adaptation, mitigation, and sustainable development. (IPCC, 2022, p. 18)

Having said that, I would like to focus on a specific business approach: "green entrepreneurship." These enterprises are designed, from their inception, to address environmental and social challenges, such as environmental sustainability, carbon footprint reduction, conservation of natural resources, and the promotion of responsible business practices. Green entrepreneurship is a response to the growing global awareness of the importance of sustainability and environmental responsibility in the world, providing a way to contribute to this goal, helping everyone in the process. While individual contributions are essential in terms of everyday actions and practices that can be implemented in households, when an entrepreneur incorporates environmental parameters from the outset of their business, the impact can be greater than that of an individual. The mindset of the "green entrepreneur" aims to generate a positive impact on the environment and society by creating eco-friendly products and services, implementing sustainable production practices, promoting the circular economy, or adopting clean technologies while also generating economic benefits. Like any entrepreneurial process and business idea, green entrepreneurship goes through various stages. However, questions posed by the green entrepreneur should always carry an environmental nuance – keeping in mind the goal of not generating greenhouse gas emissions and contributing to environmental solutions. Entrepreneurs are characterized by their ability to take risks, adapt to changing situations, and mobilize resources with creativity and business vision; the "green entrepreneur" does all of this with an environmentally responsible vision.

Several segments of the economy where green entrepreneurship can be established include:

• *Solar and wind energy*: Companies and projects dedicated to the generation of clean energy.

• *Recycling*: Organizations focused on the management and transformation of plastic waste into sustainable construction materials.

• *Sustainable agriculture*: Entrepreneurships centered around organic farming practices and the production of local and sustainable foods.

• *Sustainable tourism*: Tour operators promoting environmental conservation and local culture.

• *Ecological products*: Manufacturing and selling environmentally friendly and sustainable products, such as toiletries, household and office cleaning products, beauty products, among others.

• *Sustainable construction*: Solutions for sustainable construction that utilize eco-friendly materials and energy-efficient construction practices.

• *Environmental education*: Organizations contributing to environmental conservation awareness through education and experiences.

15

Legal frameworks
and security to protect the
environment

I n Latin America, environmental crimes often receive
minor and bailable sanctions. It is essential to advocate
for strengthened environmental regulations that establish
exemplary penalties. The need for implementing a balanced approach that combines incentives and penalties is
crucial. For example, in the fight against deforestation, it is
imperative to have agile and robust regulatory frameworks, accompanied by an adequate allocation of police
and prosecutorial personnel to ensure effective enforcement of sanctions. It is essential to analyze the panorama
in detail, country by country, to determine which nations
have environmental laws and punishments that truly
deter these harmful practices.

In most countries in Latin America, the absence of
robust criminal regulations is evident in matters of great

severity, such as mercury discharges into rivers and chemical contamination in tropical rainforests. Even deforestation, which until recently in Colombia was a crime with bailable penalties, must be addressed seriously and urgently. Environmental crimes should be considered as crimes against humanity, since they deeply erode long-term living conditions. In this regard, the green manifesto also advocates for the updating of the regulatory system to effectively punish these destructive behaviors.

It is important to understand that, while education and awareness are essential for changing habits in the long term, the existence of criminal structures that exploit and degrade the environment demands a robust response. Humanity must send an unequivocal message that these actions will not be tolerated. Therefore, the implementation of punitive sanctions is a necessary tool to deter those seeking to benefit at the expense of natural resources and the ecological balance. The combination of stronger environmental regulations and educational measures can catalyze a real shift towards sustainable practices and the lasting protection of our environment.

But why is the environment subject to rights? And why are actions that threaten it subject to penalization? It is interesting to note that, since 1972, with the Stockholm Declaration, the right to a healthy environment began to be recognized, and states were required to not cause harm to their own or other states' environments. Subsequent global conferences reaffirmed these agreements, increased nations' responsibility towards the environment, and created frameworks for its protection. Unfortunately, it seems that all of this has been insufficient.

Currently, there is a growing recognition that nature, in all its forms and ecosystems, possesses intrinsic value and an inherent right to exist, flourish, and evolve in its natural state. These rights are fundamental because they acknowledge that nature is not merely a resource for human exploitation but an entity with dignity and inherent value deserving legal protection. In a way, this ancestral view of respect for nature has been reaffirmed by contemporary law, which understands that resources are finite, and that resource use cannot be synonymous with destruction.

Recognizing Earth and the environment as subjects of legal rights imposes responsibilities on humans and governments to protect and preserve these rights. This includes the obligation to prevent environmental harm, promote the restoration of degraded ecosystems, and ensure that human activities are conducted sustainably and respectfully towards nature. It also involves employing law enforcement, judicial, and punitive mechanisms to punish offenders.

Harming nature is considered a crime because it involves damaging or destroying the inherent rights of the Earth and the environment. This can include, among other things:

- Illegal deforestation
- Illegal mining
- Promotion and financing of both illegal deforestation and mining
- Wildlife trafficking
- Illicit handling and use of genetically modified organisms, microorganisms, and hazardous substances or elements
- Pollution of rivers and seas
- Poaching of endangered species
- Air pollution
- Illegal fishing
- Illegal dumping of chemical waste into rivers
- Unsustainable agriculture, including excessive pesticide use and soil degradation
- Unregulated extraction of natural resources, such as overfishing and unsustainable logging.

These actions not only cause immediate harm to ecosystems and biodiversity, but they also have long-term repercussions on human health and the stability of the planet. The legality of these acts varies according to the specific laws and regulations of each country, but internationally, several treaties and agreements, such as the Convention on Biological Diversity and the Kyoto Protocol, establish norms and principles advocating for environmental protection.

Particularly in Colombia, the 1991 Political Constitution stands out for safeguarding environmental rights and citizens' duties towards nature. In fact, Colombia has witnessed significant legal milestones reflecting this spirit, such as the recognition of the Atrato and Cauca rivers and the Pisba *paramo* as legal subjects, to name a few examples.

16

The participation of indigenous communities in environmental protection

The essayist and religious scholar, Karen Armstrong, wrote "Sacred Nature" (2022), a profound reflection on the historically varied relationships that humans have had with nature. According to the author, in general, Eastern and indigenous beliefs have regarded humans and nature as a single entity. In contrast, Western, rational, and pragmatic conceptions, including religions such as Catholicism or Judaism, started viewing nature as something destined for human use and exploitation. In other words, while in Eastern and indigenous perspectives, God or deities (whichever they may be) were present in all things, leading to unquestionable respect and infinite reverence for natural resources, in Western religious views, God was "confined" to the heavens and seen as a separate entity from the earthly realm.

By rationalizing nature and confining God to the heavens, we have drastically reduced the divine to the point where many see it as imperceptible or unworthy of belief. Simultaneously, in our modern industrialized societies, we have systematically proceeded with the destruction of the natural order. By forcing the natural world to enhance our lives without recognizing the sanctity of its essence, we have damaged it, perhaps irreparably. On the other hand, by excluding the cultured veneration of nature from our conception of the divine, we have developed an unnatural perception of God. (Armstrong, 2022)

This desacralization of the Earth, continues Armstrong, has made us feel no compassion for the planet and its resources. Consequently, its exploitation up until now has been without any thought for the wounds inflicted. We are now living in a moment of awareness towards the sacredness of the planet, and the focus is on respecting it. However, as we have pointed out, the path is long and requires a lot of education, changes in habits, creativity, and innovation to alter deeply ingrained behaviors. "If today we have come to understand that devotion to the planet requires an adherence to the whole of things and beings that inhabit it, we must admit that this worldview dates back to the very origins of humanity," notes Armstrong (2022).

Indeed, for centuries, this depletion of natural resources worldwide has also involved the marginalization of the sacred vision held by the primary, original, and indigenous cultures that populated most of the Earth's territories. It has overlooked something about Indigenous Peoples and Local Communities (IPLC), highlighted by the report *Best Practice in Delivering the 30x30 Target*:

> The 30x30 target is only achievable if the rights and territories of IPLCs are fully integrated. IPLCs hold at least half the world's land, much of it under customary tenure. Indigenous Peoples have tenure rights on at least 38 million hectares, or a fifth to a quarter of the land surface, including ~40% of terrestrial protected areas and ecologically intact landscapes, and at least 36% of intact forests (Dudley & Stolton, 2022, p. 28).

The full and effective participation of indigenous peoples and local communities is crucial because they possess diversified knowledge systems that promote active and collective conservation. However, to achieve successful management, it is necessary to address issues such as land ownership security, inter-institutional collaboration, and overcoming historical tensions between governments and indigenous peoples. This raises crucial questions about how indigenous peoples can be more effective in biodiversity conservation in their territories, how they wish to integrate their management systems with broader conservation strategies, what conservation category would best support their institutions and rights, what reforms are necessary to ensure the continuity of conservation in their territories, and how much it would cost to create the conditions for this.

Additionally, it is vital to establish safeguards and standards to ensure that indigenous peoples are not adversely affected by the implementation of the 30x30 initiative; the focus should be on human rights and sustainable conservation. IPLCs are increasingly demanding more cultural recognition, and their productive and knowledge systems are seen as bastions of the effective conservation of resources through active and collective administration models, supported by the transmission of knowledge between generations. In Colombia, for example, indigenous peoples and local communities own 38.2% of the country's land, and in these areas, the carbon loss rate recorded is less than half that of other areas across the national territory.

At this point, it is crucial to highlight the fundamental role of indigenous women. They are the custodians of the culture and traditions of their communities, including the preservation of their languages, taking on the task of teaching them to children. They receive and pass down ancestral knowledge, stories, spiritual practices, and rituals to future generations. They also contribute to the sustenance of their families through agriculture, food collection, and artisanal production. Additionally, they are often the primary caregivers for children and the elderly. Their political participation and leadership are essential as they actively participate in political decision-making and advocate for the recognition of their rights and representation in government institutions. They have become prominent defenders of the environment, as a result of the aforementioned roles. Their resistance and activism for human rights and indigenous rights have been met with discrimination, violence, and marginalization. Indigenous women are often responsible for maintaining social and community cohesion. This participation has undoubtedly been essential for asserting that:

> There is evidence that terrestrial and marine areas under the control of Indigenous Peoples or other community management undergo less vegetation change (such as deforestation or forest degradation) than elsewhere, and sometimes do better than state-run protected areas. For example, a study of community forests in 51 countries found environmental conditions increased in 56% and decreased in 32%. Adaptive, place-based, and local governance of resources provides a powerful mechanism for achieving effective and socially just environmental stewardship. Ecosystem recovery is evident in many Locally Managed Marine Areas, and Indigenous Peoples have major roles in managing inland wetlands. Traditional ecological knowledge and management inform conservation, making it important to integrate such knowledge

and experience into management strategies. A systematic review found conservation projects with Indigenous Peoples in a strong decision-making role are consistently more successful than those in the hands of outside groups that seek to supersede customary institutions. The conditions for mitigation of climate change are also improved. Yet poorly managed, top-down, externally driven conservation approaches are still often applied leading to or exacerbating conflicts that obstruct conservation effectiveness over the long term. (Dudley & Stolton, 2022, p. 28).

Some successful cases of environmental conservation projects led by indigenous groups in Latin America include:

• *Maya Biosphere Reserve, Guatemala*: Mayan indigenous groups in Guatemala have been involved in the conservation of the Maya Biosphere Reserve, a vast area comprising 21,602 km² of tropical rainforest that is home to vast riches of biodiversity. They have worked on the sustainable management of natural resources and the protection of critical areas for biodiversity.

• *Isiboro Secure Indigenous Territory and National Park (TIPNIS), Bolivia*: Indigenous peoples in Bolivia, such as the Mojeños-Trinitarios and Yuracarés, have been actively involved in protecting TIPNIS, an area of 13,722 km² with significant biodiversity in the Bolivian Amazon. They have fought against threats such as deforestation and road construction.

• *Sian Ka'an Biosphere Reserve, Mexico*: The Mayan people of the Yucatán Peninsula have participated in the management of the Sian Ka'an Biosphere Reserve, a 5,281 km² area declared a UNESCO World Heritage Site. They have been involved in conserving the jungle, wetlands, and coral reefs in the area.

• *Indigenous Territories in the Amazon, Brazil*: Various indigenous groups in Brazil, including the Kayapó and Yanomami, have been fighting for decades to protect their territories in the Amazon. They have been key advocates for the rainforest and have worked to combat deforestation and illegal mining. Indigenous lands total 1,179,001 km².

• *Río Plátano Biosphere Reserve, Honduras*: Miskito and Garifuna indigenous groups in Honduras have actively participated in the conservation of the 5,300 km² Río Plátano Biosphere Reserve, a UNESCO World Heritage Site. They have worked to preserve the biological and cultural diversity of the region.

Traditional practices, such as the *chagra* (complex agroforestry system developed by indigenous communities), common among groups in Colombia, Ecuador, and Venezuela, have demonstrated a positive impact on environmental conservation. The *chagra* involves cultivating sustainably managed plots that integrate a variety of local crops, fruit trees, and medicinal plants. It serves as an example of agroecology and ancestral agriculture, promoting biodiversity and preserving natural resources. In addition to being a food source, the *chagra* is also a symbol of indigenous culture and their connection with the land and nature. It acts as a focal point around which families and groups gather based on kinship or affinity.

Indigenous groups are also known for their impressive adaptability and resilience. For centuries, they were victims of exploitation, expropriation, or displacement, but laws and nations are now acknowledging them and attempting to return their original land and respect their rights. Reparations, relocations, and public acknowledgments have been made to restore their dignity. For indigenous communities, everything the land provides is part of their vision of the universe and maintains a sacred position in their belief system. This spurs their natural inclination to preserve and care for nature. It is essential to protect their traditions and their culture so that their legacy can contribute to the current efforts of environmental preservation. In conclusion, I would like to once again quote Karen Armstrong:

If we allow nature into our lives, it can permeate our minds and become a formative influence. We can begin by taking very simple steps, perhaps sitting for ten minutes a day in a garden, without headphones or mobile phones, simply contemplating the views and listening to the sounds of nature. Instead of taking photos of everything around us, we should observe the birds, flowers, clouds, and trees and let them imprint themselves on our minds. (2022)

Nature has never left the lives of indigenous populations in Latin America: efforts must be made to prevent the dynamics of urban life from changing that. For those of us who are not part of these groups, we should try to incorporate their perspectives into our environmental education in order to create harmony with the environment from a spiritual standpoint. This, in combination with technical and scientific advancements, could lay the groundwork for a new wave of citizens – one that is more aware, more active, and a protagonist in this essential change.

17

Biodivercitizens: a movement with new ethics

I t is essential to base our policies on solid research that reflects citizen behaviors and their impact on the environment. We need a new civic pact, clear rules for everyone that provide us with a clearer vision of the challenges we face and allow us to design effective strategies for building a sustainable future.

A significant proportion of citizens in Latin America still do not have a full understanding of the effects of climate change on the region. This lack of awareness highlights the need to intensify educational and communication efforts in order to keep the population informed about the climate risks and the importance of collective action.

We do not need a detailed analysis to see that the consumer patterns in the region still rely heavily on single-use products and plastic packaging, which lead to heavy contamination of our ecosystems. It is essential to promote the reduction of single-use plastics and encourage recycling, as well as to adopt responsible consumer practices. In this regard, packaging producers can play a key role in reducing the supply of non-recyclable packaging and replacing it with environmentally friendly materials. In doing so, they will provide end consumers with more options in the market.

There is a connection between environmental degradation and social vulnerability in Latin America. The poorest and most marginalized populations are also those most affected by the loss of ecosystems and extreme weather events. This underlines the need for inclusive approaches that simultaneously deal with social justice and environmental protection.

On the path towards a more sustainable and resilient future, each of us plays an important role. Adopting conscious habits can make a significant difference towards reducing greenhouse gas emissions and mitigating the impacts of global warming. Before buying something – a product or a service – we should always think about the environmental implications of that purchase.

Responsible energy management is fundamental. Switching off lights and electronic devices when we are not using them, as well as making use of natural light, reduces energy consumption. Equally, choosing renewable energy to power homes and businesses helps reduce our reliance on fossil fuels.

Climate change is also linked to our eating habits. Reducing our consumption of meat and animal by-products, especially those involving intensive production practices, can reduce our carbon footprint and the deforestation associated with agriculture. We can also seek out producers that have been certified for emission control.

Reducing, reusing, and recycling are actions that make all the difference. Avoiding single-use products and opting for reusable products reduces the generation of plastic waste and contributes to the conservation of natural resources.

Awareness regarding water use is essential. Avoiding waste and adopting practices geared towards saving water, such as fixing leaks and using efficient irrigation systems, are fundamental measures for conserving this vital resource.

Encouraging participation in environmental education and awareness programs can help increase our knowledge of the effects of climate change. Being clued up on the challenges and available solutions allows us to make informed decisions in our daily lives.

In such a fragmented and polarized world, it is a massive achievement for us to agree as a society that we must stop climate change, and that a vital contribution to this objective lies in the hands of normal citizens. Their acts and decisions within their local sphere of influence can help to mitigate the impact of global warming. As Paul Hawken points out, when quoting Bill McKibben (one of the first authors to write a book about climate change, in

1989): "Movements only take 5 or 10% of people to become decisive, because, in a world where apathy reigns, 5 or 10% is a huge number" (2017). And he finishes by saying: "Movements are dreams with hands and feet, hearts and voices" (Hawken, 2017). Let's dream of a zero emissions Latin America where we produce while conserving and conserve while producing, with low carbon societies and economies that have a positive relationship with nature. And then let's make this a reality. Our future is at stake, but, more than ever, it is also in our own hands.

Our individual manifesto

This *green manifesto* has been an invitation to the Global South, from a perspective that is particularly applicable to Latin America and the Caribbean. If our implementation is rapid and dynamic, countries will be carbon neutral and net zero within the established timeframes. This effort requires an enormous commitment from states, policymakers, the private sector and each one of us as individuals in civil society.

It is true that the great global commitments are made by nations, but we cannot fool ourselves: if climate action does not start with each one of us individually, we will not be able to achieve anything. Our own manifesto as human beings demands awareness, determination and a new concept of ethics and urban living. Do we know what our individual emission levels are? Have we calculated our carbon footprint? These crucial questions should make us more aware of who we are and how we can better become integral members of a society that is fighting to avoid a climate disaster that will slowly make us extinct.

If we want to achieve the results of the green manifesto, we need to make our contribution as individuals. Let's follow the concept of recycling, reducing, and reusing in our homes and workplaces; let's be rational with our use of water and efficient with our electricity consumption, starting by switching off lights that we are not using; let's use bicycles more or walk for short trips, let's use carpooling services or public transportation; let's reduce the consumption of certain foods that put pressure on our ecosystems; let's plant trees as a habit; let's use LED lighting; let's consume products known for their environmental and ethical visions; let's reject products that have a negative impact on the environment and do not make steps to reduce their carbon footprint; and let's spend time educating ourselves and others about conservation. These are just some of the actions within our reach and that depend solely on us and our discipline.

We cannot merely be spectators of major environmental summits and expect the nations that have polluted the planet the most to take responsibility. We must be proactive and assess how we can increase our use of unconventional renewable energy, how we can transition to electric vehicles, and how we can protect species and underground aquifers. These tasks should be our motivation in a world that seems to gallop ceaselessly towards technological transformations.

Let's sign this manifesto with ourselves, our loved ones, our friends, and our surroundings. Let's love nature more, understand how it operates, and what it requires from us; let's demand global action, but let's also be effective with our local actions. We should understand that our common home needs us, demands the best of us, and is warning us. Never before have we seen so many climate migrants, so many victims of extreme heat, so many direct threats with natural disasters, floods, droughts, and extreme events. Let's not stop or be indifferent or passive in the face of this situation.

The effective combination of this *green manifesto* and our individual manifesto will bring faster results, give us the legitimacy to make demands without hesitation and ensure that no climate action can or should be threatened by ideological prejudices.

Our role on Earth is to preserve our common home, Mother Nature, to be able to apologize for years of making a constant detrimental impact in the name of growth, and to do so with a 21st-century ethical system that demands accountability from the state, consistently and coherently.

We are *biodivercitizens* and we belong to the generations that have the unavoidable task of saving the planet from irreversible consequences. No more discussions, it's time to act. The future generations expect no less from us.

My greatest motivation for this book, for the path I have taken for the environment and climate action, are my children. Every action I take and each proposal I explore is done with them in mind, as well as all future generations who will have to face and adapt to climate challenges. Today's generations are those who have suffered the consequences of so many years of unchecked emissions, but we are also the last generations that can do something to stop an even greater catastrophe. Doing this successfully will involve governments, companies, organizations, and individuals. It requires humility on our part, as well as determination and, above all, the obligation to take on a different role in our lives and with our consumption habits. We cannot shrink before this challenge of our time, so let's forge forwards for our present and OUR FUTURE.

Iván Duque Márquez

Nairobi, Kenya, September 2023

ACKNOWLEDGMENTS

This book is the result of plenty of teamwork and interaction with a lot of people over the last year. I would, therefore, like to thank Juanita Escallón and Luis Fernando Páez, who have been fundamental in contributing with their experience as editors and helping give my research, conferences and technical writings – which make up the body of thinking and doctrine of the green manifesto – a fresh tone and flow. Of course, this project would not be possible without the support of Carlos Mendoza and his graphic contribution. I thank him and Felipe Coral, my principal advisor, as well as my assistant, Deisy Moreno, and Soraya Yanine, my Communications Director. I'd also like to thank Andrés Agudelo, my digital advisor, for helping me organize the texts and interviews, as well as systematizing all the chats and ideas on the material I have been developing in different places around the world.

I also want to thank the Blavatnik School of Government at the University of Oxford, and especially the dean, Ngaire Woods, and Professor Karthik Ramana, for motivating and supporting me with this book during my fellowship in this great knowledge laboratory. I also want to express my gratitude to Sergio Diazgranados, President of the Development Bank of Latin America (CAF), for supporting this research, its publication, and dissemination.

I would also like to thank Luigi Echeverri, Carlos Eduardo Correa, María Paula Correa, Víctor Muñoz, Diego Mesa, Carlos Alvarado, George Logothetis, Juan Pablo Bonilla, Andrew Steer, Christian Samper, M. Sanjahan, Ani Dasgupta, Mathew Swift, Kartik Jaram, Daniel Pacthod, Bob Sternfels, Mark Green, Eddy Acevedo, Carlos Díaz Rosillo, Luis Amaral, Jane Goodall, Alan Fleischman, Tito Crisien, Joseph Ngaga, Russ Feingold, Brian Odonell, Zach Goldsmith, Antonio José Ardila, Gabriel Gilinski, David Vélez, Carlos Córdoba, Pedro Miguel Estrada, and Tito Crissien, with whom I have had the opportunity to discuss and test many of the ideas expressed in this book.

My gratitude also goes to Editorial Planeta, especially to Bayardo Henao, who was always enthusiastic about this project, and Mariana Marczuk, editorial director, who always saw the need to make this book accessible to readers.

In this work, my main collaborators have been my wife, María Juliana; my children, Luciana, Matías, and Eloísa, and my brother, Andrés, who were the first to make comments and suggestions on how to connect an environmental vision with practical impact measures.

In general, this manifesto is a testimony of gratitude to all those who, through different professions and activities, dedicate their lives to protecting the planet. You are my inspiration.

BIBLIOGRAPHY

Aguayo, M. (2023, 22 August). Del calentamiento global a la "ebullición global": el porqué del lenguaje sobre el clima. *El País.* https://n9.cl/6k2sx

Armstrong, K. (2022). *Sacred Nature: Restoring Our Ancient Bond with the Natural World.*

Chamon, M., Klok, E., Thakoor, V., & Zettelmeyer, J. (2022). *Debt-for-Climate Swaps: Analysis, Design, and Implementa- tion.* International Monetary Fund. https://n9.cl/3xrk8

De la Rosa, M. (2022). *Carbon credits: What are they and what have been some of the issues with their application?* Blog. https:// n9.cl/vqxlx

Deloitte. Point of View. (2022). *Mercados voluntarios de car- bono. Claves para su desarrollo en América Latina.* https:// n9.cl/naepq

Dudley, N., & Stolton, S. (Eds.). (2022). *Best Practice in Delivering the 30x30 Target Protected Areas and Other Effective Area-Based Conservation Measures* (2. ed.). The Nature Conservancy and Equilibrium Research. https://n9.cl/v49l8

Duque Márquez, I. (2021). *The road to zero.* Planeta.

DW. (2023, 20 de September). *Crisis del clima abrió "puertas del infierno", dice Guterres.* https://n9.cl/vbees

ECLAC news. (2009). *Desastres naturales causan cerca de US\$7 mil millones en pérdidas materiales al año.* https://n9. cl/6g6bf

El Ágora. (2020, 17 de April). *Europa impulsa un marco común para inversiones verdes.* https://n9.cl/ich9d

Gates, B. (2021). *How to avoid a climate disaster.* Plaza & Janés. Georgieva, K., Chamon, M., & Thakoor, V. (2022). *Swapping Debt for Climate or Nature Pledges Can Help Fund Resilience.* IMF Blog. https://n9.cl/jtd7g

Glemarec, Y. (2011). *Catalysing Climate Finance: A Guidebook on Policy and Financing Options to Support Green, Low-Emission and Climate-Resilient Development* United Nations Development Programme. https://n9.cl/xaji2d

Global CCS Institute. (2020). *Net-Zero and Geospheric Return: Actions Today for 2030 and Beyond.* https://n9.cl/x90qx

Hawken, P. (2017). *Drawdown. The Most Comprehensive Plan Ever Proposed to Reverse Global Warming.* Penguin Books. Herrán, C. (2012, 28 November). *The path towards a green economy.* Friedrich Ebert (FES) Foundation Climate and Energy Project. https://n9.cl/ef2q4 Intergovernmental Panel on Climate Change (IPCC). (2022).

Inter-American Development Bank (IDB) (2022, 10 November). *IDB, Green Climate Fund Endorse Program to Promote E-Mobility in Latin America, Caribbean.* https://n9.cl/hadfo

Intergovernmental Panel on Climate Change (IPCC). (2023). *Climate Change 2023: Synthesis Report.* [Contribution of Wor- king Groups I, II and III to the Sixth Assessment Report of the Intergovernmental Panel on Climate Change. Core Writing Team, H. Lee and J. Romero (eds.). IPCC, Geneva, Switzer- land, pp. 35-115, doi: 10.59327/IPCC/AR6-9789291691647]. https://ipcc.ch/report/ar6/syr/

Intergovernmental Panel on Climate Change (IPCC). *Climate Change 2022: Impacts, Adaptation and Vulnerability.* [Contribution of Working Group II to the Sixth Assessment Report of the Intergovernmental Panel on Climate Change [H.-O. Pörtner, D.C. Roberts, M. Tignor, E.S. Poloczanska, K. Mintenbeck, A. Alegría, M. Craig, S. Langsdorf, S. Löschke,

International Finance Corporation, World Bank. (2023). *Colombia: report on climate and development in the country.* https://n9.cl/5td81

International Monetary Fund (IMF). (2021). *Economic Outlook: The Americas: A long and winding road to recovery.* https://n9.cl/972ad

Invemar. (2010). *Siembra y restauración de corales en el Parque Nacional Natural Tayrona.* https://n9.cl/vo8ny

Lacy-Niebla, M. (2021). Climate change and the COVID-19 pandemic. *Arch Cardiol Mex, 91*(3), 269-271. https://n9.cl/19fwr

Mora, D. (2021, 17 August). *Cambio climático: América Latina será una de las regiones más afectadas.* United Nations. UN News. https://n9.cl/zxdtt

Pacific Marine Environmental Laboratory (PMEL). (2022). *International State of the Climate in 2021 Released: record- high greenhouse gases, ocean heat content, and global sea level.* https://n9.cl/508bo

Pan American Health Organization (PAHO) & World Health Organization (WHO). Sustainable Food Systems for Healthy Diets. https:// shorturl.at/aiuzJ

Pan American Health Organization (PAHO) & World Health Organization (WHO). (s. f.). *Climate change and health.* https://n9.cl/g0ocs

Studer, I. (2019, 18 August). *Latin America's Natural Resources and Climate Change.* The Nature Conservancy. https:// n9.cl/izmhn

Suárez Londoño, M. F. (2022, 25 October). *Sin energía no hay potencia mundial de la vida.* El País. https://n9.cl/9x7pw

United Nations (UN). (s. f.). *The Paris Accord.* https://n9.cl/6fvhk

United Nations Economic Commission for Latin America and the Caribbean (ECLAC). (2009). *Climate Change and Development in Latin America and the Caribbean. Overview 2009.* ECLAC. https://shorturl.at/dtADX

United Nations Economic Commission for Latin America and the Caribbean (ECLAC). Sustainable Development and Human Settlements Area. (2010). *Methods for calculating the carbon footprint and its potential implications for Latin America.* ECLAC. https://n9.cl/eqltk

United Nations Economic Commission for Latin America and the Caribbean (ECLAC). (2021). *Forest loss in Latin America and the Caribbean from 1990 to 2020: the statistical evidence.* https://hdl.handle.net/11362/47151

United Nations Economic Commission for Latin America and the Caribbean (ECLAC). (2022). *Launch event for the Sustainable Finance Taxonomies for LAC Group.* [Event]. https://n9.cl/pck68

United Nations Economic Commission for Latin America and the Caribbean (ECLAC). (2022, 22 July). *The World Meteorological Organization presents the Report on the State of Climate in Latin America and Caribbean* [Press release]. https://n9.cl/wtir2

United Nations Economic Commission for Latin America and the Caribbean (ECLAC). (2023, 10 July). *Foreign Direct Investment in Latin America and the Caribbean Rose by 55.2% in 2022, Reaching a Historic High* [Press release]. https:// n9.cl/who59

United Nations Environment Programme (UNEP) & World Conservation Monitoring Centre (WCMC) (2016). *The state of biodiversity in Latin America and the Caribbean: a mid-term review of progress towards the Aichi biodiversity targets.* https://n9.cl/rbhx9

United Nations Environment Programme (UNEP) (s. f.). *Nationally determined contributions (NDC). The Paris Accord and nationally determined contributions.* https://n9.cl/bum3p

United Nations Environment Programme (UNEP). (2022). *Emissions Gap Report 2022. The Closing Window - Climate Crisis Calls for Rapid Transformation of Societies.* Nairobi. https://n9.cl/cny9ym

United Nations Population Fund (UNFPA). (s. f.). *Supporting the generation of opportunities for those at the center of the development agenda.* https://n9.cl/6d0oh

V. Möller, A. Okem, B. Rama (eds.)]. Cambridge University Press. Cambridge University Press, Cambridge, UK and New York, NY, USA, doi:10.1017/9781009325844.]. https:// n9.cl/0crt7k

World Bank. (2022). *A roadmap for climate action in Latin America and the Caribbean world bank group 2021-2025.* https://n9.cl/q39ig

World Bank. (2022, 14 September). *The World Bank calls for urgent climate action in Latin America and the Caribbean to accelerate the transition to resilient and low-carbon economies* [Press release]. https://n9.cl/gckp1

World Bank. (2022, 3 November). *Countries Could Cut Emissions by 70% by 2050 and Boost Resilience with Annual Investments of 1.4% of GDP* [Press release]. https://n9.cl/8wmka

World Meteorological Organization. (2021). *State of the Climate in Latin America & the Caribbean 2020.* https://n9.cl/uhwpr

236